Emigration to and from the German-Russian Volga Colonies

DARREL PHILIP KAISER

Published October 2007
by Darrel P. Kaiser

Darrel Kaiser Books
www.DarrelKaiserBooks.com
email:Dar-Bet@att.net

Second Edition

ISBN 978-0-6151-7010-7

The Author

Darrel P. Kaiser has been researching the development of the Germanic peoples and his ancestors for over 10 years. While living in Bavaria and Germany for over two years, he "walked the lanes" and did on-site research in the villages of his ancestors.

He has also been professionally troubleshooting electrical, electronic, and mechanical components and systems for the US Government for the last 37 years. During those years, Darrel also trained with *PFAFF* in Germany and *BERNINA* USA in the art of professional sewing machine repair, and continues repair and restoration even today.

After all those years of troubleshooting and repair, he turned to teaching at a Government University and writing technical books. Out of his research came his first book on Germanic History and Genealogy, "*Origins and Ancestors Families Karle & Kaiser of the German-Russian Volga Colonies.*"

Darrel has also written and published numerous other books on German and Russian History, Politics, Religion, and Ancestry; a book on the Watercolor quilts of Betty Kaiser, a book on basic electrical troubleshooting, a book on sewing machine troubleshooting, two books on the SINGER 221 *Featherweight*, and two books on the

STANDARD *Sewhandy* and GE *MODEL A* sewing machines. This book's final pages show all the titles.

For more on his research into German and Russian History and Genealogy, visit his website at
www.Volga-Germans.com

For more on his books on Troubleshooting, visit his website at
www.BasicTroubleshooting.com

For more on his books about Sewing Machines, visit his website at
www.SewingMachineTech.com

For more on his books about the STANDARD *Sewhandy* and GE *MODEL A* sewing machines, visit his website at
www.SewhandySewingMachines.com

For more information on all of his books, visit his website at
www.DarrelKaiserBooks.com

Preface

This book describes the movement of the Volga Germans starting with their emigration from Germany to Russia in the 1760's. After 75 years, some of the settlers migrated west of the Volga Colonies in a search for more farm lands. In the 1870's, more Volga German-Russians left the Colonies and immigrated to Brazil in South America. Brazil did not work out well, and the South America emigration moved south to Argentina where the land was more fertile. As Moscow clamped down in the late 1800's and early 1900's on the Volga German-Russians, many thousands left land and homes for the United States and Canada

Stalin ordered the "forced emigration" or deportation of all the German-Russians of the Volga Colonies in the early 1940's. This movement scattered the remaining Volga German-Russians across Siberia, Kazakhstan, Kirghiztan, and other places.

This book documents the events and actions that led up to the deportation of the German-Russians from the Volga Colonies, and the horrible conditions they endured as they attempted to survive in Siberia and other areas as "less than human beings." Also discussed is the retraction of charges by Krushchev and the Soviet Government that led to the German-Russians release from their exile, and the eventual realization that they are a "People" with no homeland.

This is my 5th book in a series on the History, Religion, Politics, and Ancestry of the German-Russians of the Volga Colonies. Some of the other books I have written on the Volga Colonies are:

"Origin & Ancestors Families Karle & Kaiser of the German-Russian Volga Colonies"

"Religions of Germany and the German-Russian Volga Colonies"

"The Bad and Downright Ugly of the German-Russian Volga Colonies"

"Moscow's Final Solution: The Genocide of the German-Russian Volga Colonies"

I have also written and published books on other topics:

"The BettyQuilts Picture Book"

"Basic Electrical Troubleshooting for Everyone"

The Featherweight Patents

The Featherweight Ads

Before the Featherweight - *Sewhandy*

For more information about my books, please visit my websites at

www.DarrelKaiserBooks.com

www.Volga-Germans.com

Your comments and/or submissions to improve this book will always be appreciated. Discussions as to the validity of my theories and assumptions are welcome. Submission of copies of photographs or documents that are applicable to the subject is encouraged, and credit will be given in the next edition.

Contact me with any and all comments and questions by email at

Dar-Bet@att.net

I sincerely hope you find this book interesting and educational! I did.

Table of Contents

Table of Contents

Chapter 1
The Long Trip

The emigration to Russia in the 1760's was long and difficult for the German Colonists heading for the Volga Colonies. They had to pack up what little they could carry and travel by river and overland to the port city of Lübeck on the northeastern coast of Germany. They might also have gone west to the port city of Rotterdam on the Netherland coast.

North
Sea

Baltic
Sea

•St Petersburg

Moscow•

Rotterdam

Lubeck

HESSEN

Frankfurt

BADEN

BAYERN

WUERTEMBERG

Emigration Itinerary

1) Central Germany overland or by river either North to Hannover and then Lubeck, or West to Rotterdam

2) Travel the NorthSea by packet ship from Rotterdam to the Baltic Sea, or from Lubeck to the Baltic Sea, and then North to St Petersburg

3) Process in Russia

Path of Emigration to Lübeck and St Petersburg [1]

Once in Lübeck, the colonists had to wait a long time due to the large crowds. The wealthier emigrants were given housing by Commissioner Schmidt in one of the nearby homes, and probably lived fairly comfortably.[2]

Most of the colonists were probably very poor and had to live in large crowded and smelly barracks. These were originally the Wulf warehouses near the city, or other warehouses near the Holstein Bridge. They were buildings without stoves, drafty, and with straw on the floor,[3] and warehouses near the harbor. The barracks were overcrowded, filthy, disease spreading, rodent infested and filled with undesirables who wanted to take advantage of, and exploit anyone they could.[4]

The unexpected and overwhelming response to Catherine the Greats' Manifesto was most apparent in Lübeck. Thousands waited there to leave as early as 1765. While waiting, the colonists received daily allowances dependant on gender and age. Men received eight, women five, children three and infants one schilling a day.

Dependable men among the emigrants were picked and given temporary titles such as "sheriff" and "foreman." They had the task of distributing the money and rations. Sometimes the stay in the cities was long because of weather and climatic conditions, frozen rivers, no money, and no room on ships.

During these extended stays, there was time for more marriages, births, and baptisms that were held at the various gathering places. Lucky for us many of the records point to the regions of origin.

This massive influx of people put a great strain on the resources of Lübeck. For a while, the city leaders opposed the housing of so many colonists moving thru the city. Eventually, the city leaders realized that all this movement brought lots of money into the city, and they became very supportive. In fact, the city authorities even aided the Recruiter agents and Russian enrollers in forcing any colonists that decided to not go to Russia to live up to their contracts.[5]

At Rotterdam, it was probably not as crowded, but they still would have had to wait their turn until it was their time to board a ship for the 1,500-mile trip over the North Sea and across the Baltic Sea to the Russian port city of St. Petersburg.

Next Stop: Kronstadt, Russia

They left on Hanseatic or English ships, or small Russian packet ships to cross the Baltic Sea. A picture of a packet ship is above.[6] Some of the vessels used could transport 280 people at a time; some were limited to much less.

Once on board, the Germans had a voyage of nine to eleven days covering about 450 miles ahead of them. In poor weather, it might take up to six weeks and water would become scarce. There were also captains who lengthened the trip unnecessarily to force the colonists to spend their travel money entirely on rations.[7]

One emigrant, Bernhard Ludwig von Platen, waited two weeks in Lübeck and then went aboard a vessel with many others. What is special about him is that he recorded his sea voyage in his poem *Travel Description of the Colonists and Russian Lifestyle of 1766-1767.* Roughly translated, his poem tells that after waiting two weeks in Lübeck, von Platen went aboard a vessel with many others. It also tells that that everyone had food (at first) and was en route to Petersburg.

The trip was made difficult by the wind and waves. The water became bad, rations gave out, their pockets were empty from purchasing provisions, and the passengers were barely fed enough to survive by the time the trip ended. This trip lasted SIX weeks. Many settlers died during these voyages.

A master baker Johannes Hühn, originally from Gelnhausen, testified in 1766 that he and the married couple Dolck and their two daughters were transported to Russia from Lübeck by a vessel belonging to Jakob Bauer. On the second day of the voyage, the daughters, whom he had come to know very well, died of a sickness that had broken out. The dead were usually put into the sea in front of the other passengers.[8]

Even on the voyages that went as planned, the colonists still suffered terribly. The ships were too small and the people were packed in as tightly as possible. One colonist wrote of his ship voyage:

"Since the majority of us had never been upon a ship, it was hard for the people to stand up because of the natural swaying of the boat. They tumbled against each other; fear and trembling mastered every mind; one cried, another swore, the majority prayed, yet in such a varied mixture that out of it all arose a strange woeful cry. Of the Catholics among us, some told there beads, one called

on this saint, another on that; the Protestants uttered pious ejaculations from the Kubach, Schmolken and other prayer books. Finally, a Catholic struck up a litany and a Lutheran the song, "beu deine Wege." And now almost the whole crowd formed two choruses of which the first sang one song, the second the other."[9]

Arrival in Kronstadt

Most of my Volga Forefathers first stepped into Russia at the port at Kronstatdt, which is part of St. Petersburg's fortifications. From there, they were moved to a village a short distance west called Oranienbaum (now called Lomonosov). Here they were given temporary housing. Each family was required to complete paperwork by the Russian Emigration.

While there, the colonists were able to obtain new clothing by using a ticket issued by their sheriff or foreman. They usually stayed around fourteen days in Oranienbaum, but their time stuck there could be indefinite. One of the mandatory requirements for continuing to the Volga was that they had to swear the oath of loyalty to the Russian Crown as set down in the 1763 Manifesto. Paragraph 5 of that document stated:

"On arrival, every foreigner intending to settle and registering themselves in the chancery set up for that purpose or in any other border town in Russia must confess his true intentions and swear an oath of loyalty according to the applicable religious ritual."

The colonists swore this oath according to their religious affiliation in Oranienbaum. They assembled in the castle chapel, with the oath being read out to them by Pastor Johann Christian König. These words were repeated by all present swearing the oath. At this point, everyone must have realized they had really become Russian subjects and return to

Germany would be impossible. Many, to keep their consciences clear and not be in breach of any future sworn oath in case they returned to Germany, as Christian Gottlieb Züge wrote:

"merely moved their lips, without saying anything."

Each colonist was also required to sign a contract that regulated all the goods and services due from the Russian side and all resultant rights and duties of each signing colonist. The contract was formal agreement between the director, Baron Caneau de Beauregard, as the delegate of Catherine II for settlement of the colonies, and each colonist. Otto Friedrich von Monjou (a second director), also occasionally appears in place of Beauregard as does the authorized director Johann Friedrich Wilhelm von Nolting zu Schloss Fauerbach near Friedberg in the Wetterau.

The agreement indicated that the colonists were already in debt to the Russian government before they ever arrived. This debt amount grew by the granting of advances during the transportation as follows: The colonist will receive for the journey from ... to St. Petersburg via Lübeck the sum of 15 Kreutzer per day, his wife 10, his children of marriageable age 10, and his minor children 6 Kreutzer per day.

This money and the payments the colonists, their heirs and/or successors may receive after arrival (an "advance" of money or things) in Catherine the Greats' domain is to be repaid after 10 years in three installments over three years. No interest is payable. The crown will also pay transport costs from St. Petersburg to the place of settlement.

In the event of departure from Russia within the next decade, only transport costs and the travel expenses subsidy to St.

Petersburg is repayable. The colonist must then also pay a fifth of all his assets acquired in the first five years after arrival to the crown. If he leaves after only six to 10 years, then only a tenth is payable. Each colonist will receive money on arrival for purchases (animals, implements, home, barn, and seed). This is also repayable. Relief from all monetary taxation and obligatory rendering of good and/or services to the Russian crown for the next 30 years is granted. The date on which debt repayment must begin will be determined later.

Other areas covered by the contract: Inheritance law was defined. Duty free import of goods to a value of 300 rubles was permitted on entry into Russia. The obligations of the Russian crown to each settler were also laid down. Freedom of religion and construction of properly built state schools for every religion. Medical services were guaranteed by the Government.

Travel out of the country was permitted, but limited by many conditions. Colonists received land (fields, pastures, woods and the like of best arable quality suited to maintain the entire family) on a hereditary leasehold basis. Colonists were in return to behave as loyal subjects of Catherine II of Russia, i.e. to adhere to Russian laws and customs, including those applying to the colonies. Annual payment of a tithe to their mayors and that mayors' right of first refusal at a price no higher than that demanded of third parties was also to be promised.

More rules included: Allocation of settlement areas on the Volga was to be in circular areas with a diameter of 60 to 70 versts (1 verst = 1.067 km) in each of which 100 families were to be settled. The number of colonies to be founded was 52 on the mountain side and 52 on the pasture side of the river. The settlers were to be allocated by confession. Each family was to be given 30 *desjatines* of land on a hereditary leasehold basis. This land could not be split up, sold or mortgaged and remained municipal property. Use of the land assigned was to be 15 *desjatines* for agriculture, 5 as pasture, 5 for dwelling and garden, plus 5 *desjatines* of woodland per family.

Inheritance - Primogeniture applied where only one son, namely the oldest, became sole heir. If he was unsuited, the father could assign it to another son or relative. The aim of this provision was:

 "to ensure that every father knowing this law would make every effort to teach all his children a trade from infancy."

Municipal self-government - Each colonist had to swear on arrival that he would adhere to the laws of the area. This legal code caused the colonists to establish themselves as a separate class with considerable privileges and freedoms (of movement, import, export, transition to another class – citizen, military, clergy, and aristocracy). The Russians called them *wolnyje ljudi*, free people. The provisions of the Colonial Law and its supplements lasted for a century, but were canceled by the Russian Government in 1871.

After swearing the oath of allegiance and signing the contract, the families were then packed onto small ships for transport to St. Petersburg. They were not given housing in the city, but were required to stay on the docked ships for as long as three weeks while at St. Petersburg.[10]

While in St. Petersburg, the colonists were given detailed descriptions of their settlement areas, all supposedly unpopulated. The officials doing so also registered all the assets each settler had with him. [11] By this time, all requirements had to be signed and completed, or they would stay indefinitely and live on the ship in deteriorating and unhealthy conditions. [12]

The Journey to Saratov

At this time, each emigrant group was assigned a Russian military leader and guards who were tasked with leading and protecting them on their trek to the Volga areas. Different routes were used. The entirely overland route went via Peterhof, Novgorod, Tver, Moscow, Riasan and Pensa to Pokrovsk (now called Engels) on the Volga, opposite Saratov.

The water route proved better for larger groups. It led from St. Petersburg by ship and moved up the Neva River and Schluesselburg Canal to Lake Ladoga, up the Volkhov River to Novgorod. Any sick people remained at Novgorod to convalesce during the winter. For those still well, the trip continued via the Msta River to Vychni Volotchok.

Overland, the route went via Torshok, Tverza, Tver and then on the Volga to Yaroslavl, Kostroma and Nishni Novgorod, ending in Saratov. The colonists traveling by water were confronted with the same treatment as on the voyage from Lübeck. Again, captains tried to lengthen the voyage to force them to spend all their allowances on overpriced provisions. Eventually, they left the ships and the river, and began following the land trail to the most northern navigable point of the Volga River at Torshok. [13]

Women and children were jammed with baggage on wagons. Men walked. The trip continued via the Msta River to Vychni Volotchok. Their goal was to reach Torshok before it became winter and cold. Some did, but some did not make it until the

October snow. Many died of exposure and illness, and were buried on the way. The goal was to go as far as possible, and they did not stop until the full winter had set in. Some were housed in Belosersk, Kyrilov, or Petrovsk. Those that reached Torshok safely usually stayed there over winter and lived with Russian peasants of near-by villages.[14]

While they were grateful to their hosts (who were being paid by the Government to house them), the Germans were amazed that their Russian hosts kept their cattle, chickens, sheep, and pigs living under the same roof with them.[15] When the Volga thawed in the Spring, they again started on their way by ship down the river towards Saratov. Some stayed on land to Kassimov to sail down the Oak River to the Volga.[16]

River damage to the ships delayed and made the travel even slower. Many died and were quickly buried on Volga riverbanks. Everyone wanted the journey to be over, and the forests along this part of the Volga was rumored to be the area of robbers and bandits.[17] They finally reached Saratov, which was the closest large city to the settlement areas.

The overland route went via Peterhof, Novgorod, Tver, Moscow, Riasan and Pensa to Pokrovsk or "Kosakenstadt" or Cossacktown (now called Engels) on the Volga, opposite Saratov. The German name for Pokrovsk was "Kosakenstadt" or Cossacktown because the town people were Cossacks.[18]

No matter how they got there, upon their arrival in Saratov, the Voevodenkanzlei (Government office) issued to them 25 to 150 Rubles, depending on how many farm animals and farm tools they were also given. They then continued to their final destinations. Grouped by destination village, those arriving in Saratov and going to the left side (Wiesenseite), moved by boat to Pokrovsk to join wagons headed south for those villages. If they arrived via Pokrovsk, then they would climb on the wagons going south.

St Petersburg

Baltic Sea

Land & River Route

Volga River

Moscow

Samara

Land Route

Volga River

Pensa

Russia

Saratov

Warenburg

Emigration Itinerary

1) Land & River Route from St Petersburg overland East to Volga River, follow Volga East to Samara, & the South to Saratov and Volga Colonies

Volgograd

Volga River

OR

2) Land Route from St Petersburg overland Southeast to Moscow & Pensa, then South to Saratov and the Volga Colonies

Path of Emigration from St. Petersburg to Saratov [19]

The distance covered was around two thousand miles. Many families took more than a year to complete the trip.

The Settlements

Settlement areas were mainly the steppes near the Volga in areas of strategic military significance to Russia. These areas were named as the governorships of Samara and Saratov. Between 1765 and 1770, 104 colonies were founded. The first founded by Protestant settlers in 1764 was named Catherinenstadt (Baronsk in Russian, later called Marxstadt). By 1772, this colony had a population of 283.

The colony founded in the same year on the mountain side of the Volga, Glaka, had 459. The Catholic colony of Mariental was founded in 1776 and had 400 inhabitants. Protestant Warenburg, founded 1767, had 592 in 1772.[20]

The Volga colony area is about 450 miles southeast of Moscow, on either side of the Volga River. Saratov was the only large Russian city in the area. The land on either side of the Volga River differed greatly, with the Bergseite (meaning hillside) or west side of the river having banks that rose steeply to a wooded hills traversed and deep gorges covered with tall grass and bushes.

The settlements of the German colonists began about thirty miles south of Saratov to nearly to Kamyshin. Only ten of the villages were near the Volga River, with all the others some distance west along smaller rivers whose waters flowed westward into the Don. Of those 104 original mother colonies, forty-five were on the Westside (Bergseite). This area corresponded to the Saratov province. Occasionally my ancestors would list the name of the province, either Saratov or Samara on their paperwork as their home instead of the name of their village.

German-Russian Volga Area

Bergseite & Wiesenseite Map [21]

Key labels on map (as visible):

Jagodnaja Poljana, Pobotachnoje, Neu-Straub, Schaffhausen, Glarus, Bettinger, Zürich, Basel, Zug, Wittmann, Schönchen, Unterwalden, Luzern, Nab, Susannental, Kind, Orlowskoje, Brockhausen, Hockerberg, Obermonjou, Fischer, Kano, Boaro, Beauregard, Katharinenstadt, Paulskoje, Rosenheim, Enders, Philippsfeld, Beckerdorf, Krasnojar, Stahl, Nieder-Monjou, Schwed, Schulz, SARATOV, Reinwald, Urbach, Reinhardt, Rohleder, Schäfer, Herzog, Pokrovsk (Engles), Graf, Marientale, Fresental, Neu-Boaro, Louis, Lilienfeld, Karanyoh, Volga River, Volga Wiesenseite, Neu-Mariental, Liebental, Alexanderhöh, Neu-Obermonjou, Weizenfeld, Neu-Urbach, Gnadendorf, Rosenfeld, Nachoi River, Neu-Laub, Brabander, Dehler, Schilling, Bangert, Stahl, Beideck, Nedemtal, Rosental, Walker, Norka, Kukkus, Lauwa, Ostenfeld, Frank Kolb, Huck, Jost, Fresenheim, Orloff, Neu-Messer, Kutter, Anton, Laub, Lindenau, Lysanderhöh, Hoffental, Neu-Donhof, Donhof, Balzer, Dinkel, Köppental, Krasnyy-Kut, Konstantinowka, New-Balzer, Messer, Straub, Brunnental, Langenfeld, Noor, Warenburg, Hussenbach, Kauz, Dietel, Merkel, Bauer, Preuss, Hussenbach, Rosenfeld, Neu-Bauer, Rothammel, Kratzke, Grinn, Hölzel, Streckerau, Gnadenfeld, Eckheim, Seewald, Degott, Solotoye, Marienberg, Neu-Beideck, Friedenfeld, Schuck, Franzosen, Seelmann, Achrenfeld, Vollmer, Husaren, Neukolonie, Jeruslan River, Pfeifer, Kanenka, Viesenmüller, Neu-Schilling, Volga Bergseite, Köhler, Hildmann, Friedenberg, Leichtling, Stephan, Müllen, Gnadentau, Senenovka, Kraft, Tscherbakovka, Goebel, Hoestein, Schwab, Dreispitz, Galka, Neu-Norka, Oberdorf, Alexandertal, Dobrinka, Erlenbach, Josefstal, Rosenberg, Marianfeld, Unterdorf, Jeruslan River, Awilowo, Ilawla River, Volga River, Kamyshin

N / W / E / S (compass)

On the Wiesenseite (meaning meadow side) or east side of the river lay a low level grassy plain, gently sloping towards the river with small slow creeks. One area of settlement began about twenty miles upstream from Saratov and continued northeastward up the Volga and eastward along both the Great and the Little Karman.

13

My ancestors' villages were in a group farther south about fifty miles downstream (Warenburg). Sixty-six mother colonies were established on the Wiesenseite.[22]

Contemplating the Volga [23]

Chapter 2
Shock & Disappointment

No one got any breaks. After the long and difficult journey, the colonists who survived were challenged with many difficulties. They were shocked when they found the real condition of land they had traveled so far to reach.

One of the Colonists, Christian Gottlieb Züge, told of the first impressions of their new land. He wrote:

"Our leader cried stop! It surprised us greatly as it was too early to camp for the night. This surprise soon changed to amazement and shock when we were told that this was our final destination. We exchanged looks of amazement at finding ourselves in a wilderness of meter-high grass with nothing else visible all around except for a small wood. None made any effort to descend from horse or wagon and as soon as we had recovered from our shock to some extent every face showed a desire to turn back. So this is the paradise promised by the Russian recruiters in Lübeck, one of my fellow sufferers exclaimed with a sad face. Admittedly, it had been stupid of us to expect an uninhabited Garden of Eden. The disappointment of finding a steppe that fulfilled none of our needs was almost unbearable. We saw no signs in the area of any attempt to welcome us in any way either then or later, although as winter was coming it seemed urgently necessary to get to work."

Züge continued in his writings that the materials that the Government had promised for house construction were not available, and all that had been done was to crudely lay out spaces for the houses. The Governments' excuse was that there were no houses built because there was no lumber available locally.

All the lumber had been ordered, but it had to be floated down the Volga River from as far away as Viatka (over 300 miles North). Once it floated as close as it could by river, the lumber still had to be dragged by horses to all the village sites.[24]

The sheer numbers of colonists evidently overwhelmed the Russians. Luckily, native Russians from surrounding villages felt sorry for the strange new people. They warned the German colonists that without adequate housing they would not survive the rapidly approaching winter.

The Russians offered to teach them how to build partially underground huts patterned after those of the some of the wild tribes living nearby.[25] These shelters, called "semlinken or semlyanka" were big enough for three or four families to live together in. With little or no ventilation and the crowded conditions, it was only adequate for their survival during the harsh Russian winters.[26]

Christian Gottlieb Züge also described the people from Lübeck he accompanied on their trek to the settlement area on the Volga. His view was not very complimentary. We should note that Züge felt that since he was a "member of an honorable trade" that he could look down on his fellow travelers (farmers and peasants) with arrogance. Züge wrote:

"Rejects who sought unknown parts since their homelands had spat them out or threatened to do so. Amoral folk able to find comfort in any situation as long as they could give their lust unbridled rein formed a second class equally unpleasant. The third class,

smallest of all, consisted of unfortunates or persecuted people. The fourth and most numerous was made up of adventurers and the easily influenced, willing to do anything if it were only sold them well enough, or inexperienced types seduced by the recruiters and who really believed mountains of gold existed as promised."[27]

History records that Christian Gottlieb Züge was never satisfied and escaped the Volga Colonies to return to Germany in 1774. While Christian Gottlieb Züge may just have been one of those people that would never be satisfied, others shared his views. One new settler wrote:

"We looked at each other with frightened expressions. We were in a wilderness without even a tree. Nothing was to be seen except the endless dry grass of the steppes."[28]

The Death Rate

The settlers felt even worse because they were homesick for Germany, for relatives they had left, and for the family members that died along the way. [29] The records do not tell us how many died during the trip from Germany to the Volga Colonies, but they do tell us that out of the 7,501 people listed on the 1766-1767 Transport Lists, an unbelievable 1,264 or 16.9% died between Oranienbaum to Saratov.

One record also tells us that approximately 6,200 (82.5%) out of the 7,501 actually made it to Saratov. The percentage that died or became lost or missing was a total of 17.5%.[30] Another record gives a slightly lower death rate of 12.5% (3,293) for the total 26,676 colonists that traveled from Oranienbaum to Saratov.[31] Even the lower number of 3,293 dead is amazing.

The Wild Weather

The climate was not anything like the recruiters promised. It was much more extreme than what was normal in Germany. The soil was salty and sandy, and good water was hard to find. Most of the colonists had fallen for the promise of good air and fertile soil in the settlement areas, like that on the upper Rhine back in Germany. They actually thought they were moving to a country something like Italy or Germany.

On the Volga, however, they found the climate to be one of wide extremes. It was nothing like what they were used to, or anything similar to Italy or Germany. Because most rain fell between October and April, their field plowing and sowing had to be deep and at the right time to guarantee the seed did not dry out. Strong winds in March and April dried the ground out.

They had to allow for late frosts that could kill the harvest. Snowstorms were common in winter causing drifts that covered the field with snow. In between the snows, there would be mild weather that melted the snow, but then the next frost turned the fields into sheets of ice. Hail showers could also ruin the crops.

The Sickness

The colonists were plagued with a sickness that killed and sometimes even wiped out entire families.[32] Some thought it was just homesickness or despair for their new life, but the fever caused many of all ages and sex to die.[33]

There was also a typhus-like sickness that usually came around in the Spring. Sometimes it also visited the people in the Fall. Records tell that in one village it struck only two months after the colonists' arrival. During the time from

September thru January, 15% of the village passed from it. Entire whole families died from this sickness.[34]

It is thought that there were three main causes for this recurring sickness. The first was the poor housing available for many of them. Those that had to build the dug-out homes (semlinken or semlyanka) to survive the cold often built in the middle of the forests or close to the riverbanks. Both locations were unhealthy. The forest air was damp and moldy. The air was made even worse inside the dug-outs with little ventilation and the crowded conditions.

Those that built near the river usually did so near the riverbends or in low places where they would be sheltered from the harsh winter winds and snows. Their plan worked and they were protected from "Old Man Winter." Unfortunately, when the snow thawed and melted in the Spring, the rivers rose and flooded their huts. This left them with absolutely nothing and nowhere to live in a village already struggling to survive.[35]

The second cause was the climate. The unexpected temperature changes in the Spring and Fall, along with the poor housing, caused the colonists to be cold more often with little resistance to sickness. Those that survived eventually did acclimatize to the weather.

The third cause was the brackish water that some of the Colonies, which were not near free running rivers, used for their drinking water supply.

Food Shortages

Another cause of the sickness could have been the shortage of food those first few years. Food was difficult to grow those first years. The land was different from back in Germany, and was even different on each side of the Volga. It took time for the farmers to learn what methods worked for growing food.

One common characteristic of many Russian rivers is that the eastern bank is flat and the other bank is steep. They called

Bergseite
(steep banks of the Volga with forested hills and deep gorges)

Medveditsa River

Rosenheim

• Katharinenstadt
Malo Karaman River

Saratov•

Bolshoi Karaman River

•Engels

• Stahl
• Kukkus   Nachoi River
•Lauwe
•Jost
•Laub Tarlyk River

Karamysh River
Norka•
Walter•   Anton•
Kutter •
Frank•   Donhof•   Balzer
Dietal•
•Grimm

. Dinkel

• Straub
•Warenburg   Krasnyy-Kut

Rothammel•
Schuck•
Medveditsa River   Vollmer•
Kamenka   Volga River
Pfeifer•
Kohler•   Kraft

Seelmann

•Holstein

Marienfeld•   Dobrinka   Jersulan River

Ilawla River

Kamyshin•

Wiesenseite
(low grassy plain sloping gently towards the Volga)

Bergseite & Wiesenseite Map [36]

20

the left bank of the Volga in the settlement area the "pasture side" and the right bank the "mountain side." The pasture side had swamp areas on the riverbanks. The fields in this flood area had thick plant growth and were used by the Volga Germans for hay and cow pastures. The bordering steppe was especially suited to wheat after having been made fit for farming. This was untamed land and it took many months to till the land. The other bank was steep with many streams.

Settlers on the flatter side had ample land to expand available, but those on the opposite bank could not expand because native Russian farmers lived on the bordering lands. Since the new Colonists did not have experience with this type of soil or climate, it would be years before they could survive on their farm harvest and production. It would take a decade before they had enough experience to be masters of the land as they had been in Germany. Until they mastered the land there was never enough food for all.

Along with the wild weather, there were hordes of mice and gophers to add to large crop losses. Soil quality, which consisted of a mountain side and a pasture side with the river in the middle, let them grow wheat, barley, watermelon, potatoes, flax and sunflowers. Woad, an herb grown for the blue dyestuff from the leaves, also grew there.

Even with all those hardships, they did eventually succeed as farmers. By 1798 (a little over thirty years since the colonies were founded), most of the colonies had at least one flourmill, a public granary, and gardens. Some even had orchards and apiaries. Most had not introduced fertilizing. They were able to grow a variety of crops to include, rye, wheat, barley, oats, millet, peas, potatoes, and tobacco.

Artisans No- Farmers Yes

The German scientist (zoologist and botanist and Professor at the St. Petersburg Academy of Science) Peter Simon Pallas wrote comments on the economic development of the Volga Colonies in his book *Journey Through the Various Provinces in Russia*, published in 1773. He also mentioned the various trades and crafts of the colonists. For many, the dream of performing their trades was not allowed. They were forced to be satisfied as farmers. As noted before, while the Recruiters would promise that a prospective colonist would be able to perform his trade, in reality what was needed and what was allowed in the Volga Colonies was only farming.

Author Gottlieb Beratz probably described it best:

"Here stood a tailor; there wigmaker; neither of them had ever harnessed a horse, not to mention worked in the fields, but nevertheless they were given an old Kalmuck horse, and a few pieces of lumber with which to make a plow and a wagon, and were calmly told to get to work."[37]

When and if the farming was finished, than the trades and crafts would be allowed to be practiced. Some villagers felt that since they had never plowed land back in Germany, they were certainly not going to do farming in the Volga Colonies. The Office of the Guardianship Chancery for Foreigners or Kontor in Saratov only had one answer for this:

"You have to become farmers now, there is no alternative."[38]

Failure to comply was "disobedience or laziness." The Kontor used the appropriate means to convince both the disobedient or lazy person to see the error of their ways.[39]

Appropriate Sign [40]

23

One of the methods that the Kontor used is explained in the following letter of October 4, 1768:

"Order to the overseer of the colony Kopenka, Nicholas Vollmar: the colonist Johannes Husz, belonging to your colony, who was condemned this past summer, for his laziness and bad management of his farm, to work in the brick factory in the colony Rossoshi, which work is now finished, is being sent back to you in the custody of a Cossack, with the instruction that he be put to work by you and that you keep him incessantly and exactly under observation. You are to report to the Kontor that he has been brought to you." [41]

Those that did not see the error of their ways after a term of forced labor in a "brick factory," earned the opportunity of serving time in the penitentiary in Saratov.[42] Most faced with this option wisely became farmers...

Typical Russian Prison [43]

Chapter 3
Emigration for More Land

Life had become better in the Colonies. The settlers had finally figured out the climate and soil, the robbers and indigenous natives had settled down, and the Russian Government was not interfering a lot. But as history has shown before, there is a down side to the good life and growth. With all their prosperity came increased population and more land was needed. So, in the 1840's a large emigration left from the Volga colonies to the Kazakhstan steppes in the southern part of the province of Samara. There a large number of settlements quickly evolved.[44]

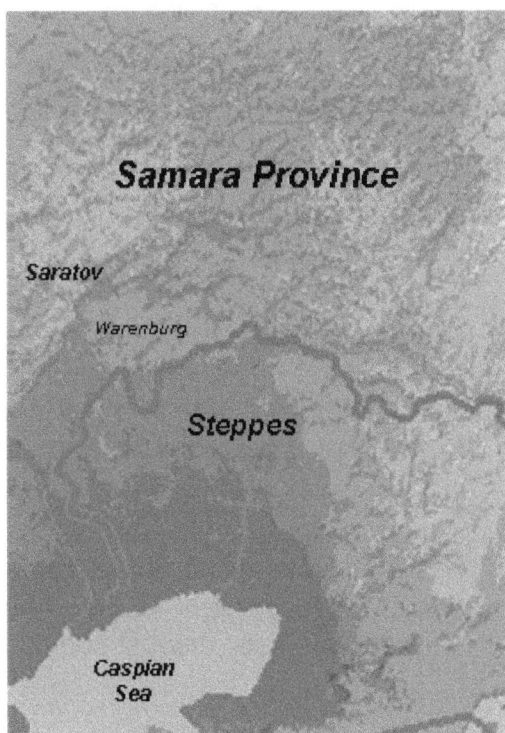

Kazakhstan Steppes [45]

Time to Leave for Anywhere Else

In 1861, Russian Tsar Alexander II emancipated all the serfs, giving them equal status with our German ancestors. This ended our ancestors "privileged status" that was granted by Catherine the Great. Ten years later in 1871, the Colonies right to self-government was ended with the nullification of the colonial law that granted it.

Three years later in 1874, their exemption from mandatory military service in the Russian Army was discontinued and men from 18 to 21 were drafted for service. The term of active military service was seven years, with another eight years in the Reserve. Many families did send their sons off to serve in the Russian army and navy.

Even today, pictures of young Volga Germans in Russian uniforms are found among our ancestral photographs.[46] It is reported that after the first young colonial men were drafted into the army, stories of their poor treatment spread along the Volga. This poor treatment included flogging for even the smallest discretions.[47]

Subsequently, thousands of twenty-year-old boys quickly decided to leave the country.[48] Their religious freedom also began to be attacked, with laws now in effect prohibiting their ownership of land unless they converted to the Orthodox faith.[49]

For many this meant the loss of all of the Tsarina Catherine the Great privileges. In the poem below, "the communist manifesto," the German colonists' disgust comes thru:

26

**"We left our native country
And pulled into the Russian
country,
The Russians were very much
beneidt us,
And because we were so long
released,
Thus Sie's brought there with
cunning,
That we no more should not be
Kolonist.
Egg Kolonisten are not we more
And must carry the rifle.
What by the envy happens
nevertheless?
One the communist manifesto
vernicht't
Originate from the German
Reich,
Now we are alike to the
Russians."** [50]

The German-Russians only had two choices. One was to stay and accept the changes, or the other was to leave. Colonists slowly began to emigrate to America and Canada, and Brazil and Argentina.

Between 1874 and 1890, it is estimated that 30,000 Germans left Russia for the new freedoms of the Americas. [51]

In 1862, a law was passed in the United States that granted land for agriculture free of charge in the recently opened west to almost all that applied. American advertising at the time pushed the idea that establishing their families in the land of the United States would make both themselves and the country better. Volga Germans eventually established themselves in Kansas, Nebraska, Colorado, Wisconsin, California, Oregon, and Washington.

Soon after the new Russian Military law took effect, a large group of Bergseite Protestants met in Balzer to discuss their future. About the same time, a large group of Catholics met in Herzog on the Wiesenseite to discuss their future.

Both groups felt that emigration was the only solution, and both chose delegations to travel to America to see if conditions for settlement and life were better there.

The groups traveled to America on the same ship in July 1974, but split up on arrival in New York and surveyed the Midwest independently. Both groups quickly returned to the Volga, and enthusiastically recommended the United States for a new life.[52]

A report about the Protestants immigrating to North America around 1874 follows:

"Among the scouting party sent to the United States by the Colonies in 1874, to seek land, were two men from Norka: Johannes Krieger and Johannes Nolde. Their reports on return soon set in motion emigration, which started as early as 1875, with seven Norka families who came to Ohio, and two years later went to Sutton, Nebraska. In 1876, one the largest Protestant groups of colonists ever to emigrate was a group of eighty-five families, most of them from Norka."

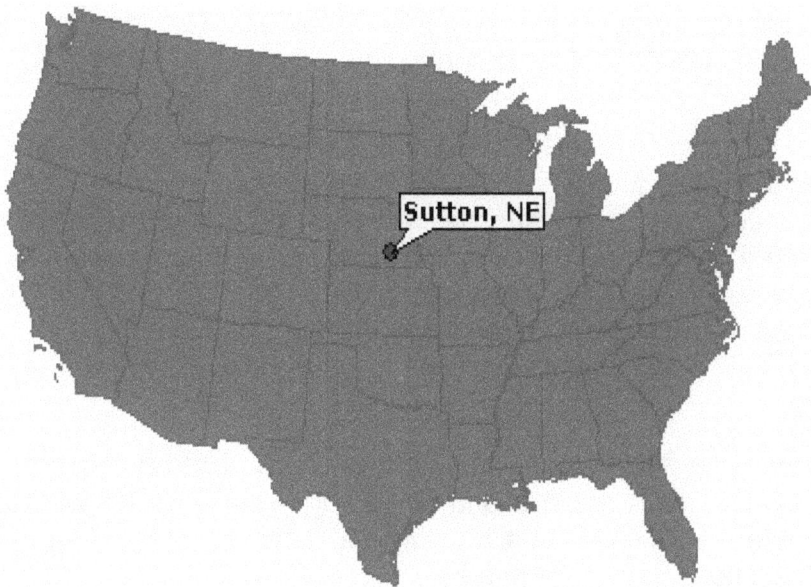

Sutton Nebraska

By the year 1920, over 300,000 first and second-generation German-Russians were living in the United States. Almost an equal amount went to Canada. This was the third and final great wave of German immigration; the first arrived in colonial times and the second, in the mid-nineteenth century.

However, the Volga German-Russians were different from those earlier German immigrants. These Germans had spent over 125 years among the Russians and their speech was interlaced with Russian words. The earlier German-Americans considered them different and did not readily accept these new German immigrants.

Along with their English-speaking neighbors, the German-Americans (who had already assimilated into the American

Society) referred to the Volga Germans as "Russians" and to their settlements as "Russian town."

As all newcomers are, they were put at the bottom of the social ladder and were forced to accept the jobs that others avoided in order to survive. Women were domestics; men worked on railroad construction, farmed, or dug ditches. They were an industrious and determined people, and all who encountered them admired their ability to work. [53]

Brazil and Argentina

There are estimates that about 250,000 German-Russians emigrated to Argentina and Brazil. [54] A large group went to southern Brazil to cultivate wheat, as they had done for generations in the Volga area.

First Brazil

Brazil was interested in the immigration of workers because slave trade was prohibited there, with a resulting shortage of available labor.

This movement started in 1876 when a large group of Catholics and Protestants from both sides of the Volga River met in Balzer to discuss possible emigration to Brazil. They had heard that the Brazilian government was willing to offer large concessions to German-Russians willing to emigrate.

A delegation of seven visited Brazil in the fall of 1876, and found land suitable for their people in the Province of Parana. [55] Brazil was ready to give to them common land sufficient to establish colonies, and granted to the immigrants the right to establish settlements of their own religion.

Travel costs, costs of the food supply during the journey, and if necessary, costs of boarding the immigrants for 12 to 20 months were to be provided by the state. The government also committed itself to finance the building of houses and build connecting roads. These negotiations resulted in accelerated preparations for emigration. Emigration transportation was arranged via a one-month sea voyage beginning usually in Hamburg.

Volga German-Russian Brazil Area
Parana Province [56]

By 1878, there were approximately 2,500 German immigrants in Brazil. However, by this time problems had begun to surface. After these reports of serious difficulties with the structure of colonies reached Russia, the enthusiasm for immigrating to this area dropped significantly.

Only after the 1887 Russian Laws tightening control of the Germans, did the emigration to Brazil increase. The year 1890 was a terrible year with food shortages in Russia. It became the high point of emigration with approximately 10,000 moving to Brazil. Today, approximately 70,000 descendants of the German-Russians in Brazil still live.

Then Argentina

Unfortunately, while the soil in Brazil was fertile, it was not the right soil for wheat. Sometime after they realized the soil problems in 1877, four representatives of the Volga Germans traveled to Buenos Aires, Argentina to negotiate with the Argentine Minister of the Interior.

The Argentine Government proposed to guarantee the immigration of 50,000. However, after the mistakes in Brazil, the colonists asked for a guarantee of good soil in order to export their agricultural products. They also asked, as their ancestors received from Russian Tsarina Catherine the Great, for exemption from military service, freedom of worship, and the installment of German schools.

The Argentine Congress agreed and confirmed the agreement by law. In December of 1877 and in January of 1878 the Volga Germans arrived in Coronel Suárez, in the province of Buenos Aires, and founded the town of Hinojo.[57] Eleven hundred Germans from the Volga area arrived in

Argentina in 1878. Further expansion out from Colonia Hinojo went westwards south of Buenos Aires into the province of La Pampa. They even eventually reached Cordoba and Chaco.

The Volga Germans also settled agricultural colonies in the Entre Ríos area. While Colonia Hinojo was the first settlement, Colonia General Alvear was the main settlement of Volga German-Russians in Argentina. Nearly 90% of the first Volga Germans that arrived in Argentina settled there.

The Colonia General Alvear was comprised of six main villages: Asunción (Spatzenkuter), Concepción (Valle María), San José (Brasilera), Agricultores (Protestante), San Francisco (Pfeifer) and Salto (Kohler). The settlers were mostly Catholic, but there was an Evangelic settlement (Protestante).

There are still fifteen villages left in the Entre Ríos that are populated by descendants of the original settlers. Of the fifteen, twelve of them are of Catholic origin with the other three Protestant.

Volga German-Russian descendants still live in small cities like Ramírez, Crespo, Urdinarrain, Galarza and Maciá. Catholic settlers in La Pampa came from south of Buenos Aires and founded Santa María and Santa Teresa. Protestants from Entre Ríos and founded Guatraché, San Martín and Alpachiri.[58]

Volga German-Russian Argentina Areas [59]

Russian Paranoia

Even as the German Colonists were leaving Russia, the Russian public was becoming even more discriminatory and paranoid. Much discussion centered on whether the original migration had been a benefit to Russia. Complete analysis of how the German Kolonisten had fulfilled their duties in comparison to their Russian neighbors. Eventually, the rational discussions were replaced with emotional nationalistic feelings of the Russian public.

This became even worse as the German Reich gained power in 1871 and moved towards its foreign policy of expansion. In the discussion around the "German question," the increasing property holdings of the German Kolonisten played an important role. In nationalistic propaganda, the Russians feared a "peaceful conquest." The Russian population feared an expansion of Germany into the German-Russian colonies.[60]

Along with the growing Russian paranoia, a terrible famine hit Russia from 1891 thru 1892. Famines were not unusual, as famines had plagued mankind in Europe and Russia throughout history. Russian Tsar Alexander I was the first Russian Monarch to attempt to create a comprehensive famine relief system in 1822. This program was modified by Tsar Nicholas I in 1834, and provided for a network of granaries. The idea was that the peasants should stock up in good years and then empty out during a crop failure. Even in the best years the peasants were too poor to contribute, and where the granaries actually existed they were usually empty.

However, the famine of 1891-1892 was particularly bad. It affected the population of an area of around 900,000 square miles in the Volga and central agricultural areas. The famine came about partially because of a recent past of poor harvests (6 of the last 12 years). Between the years of 1879 and 1889, six of the years saw poor harvests. These harvests had been negatively affected by both natural problems and by man-made circumstances (drought, population growth, poor growing seasons, and soil erosion).

The total number of deaths due to the famine of 1891-1892 was approximately 700,000.[61] Even worse, this famine affected the lives of between fourteen to twenty million people. This was another reason to leave.

Almost too Late to Leave

While there were German-Russians that left the Volga area

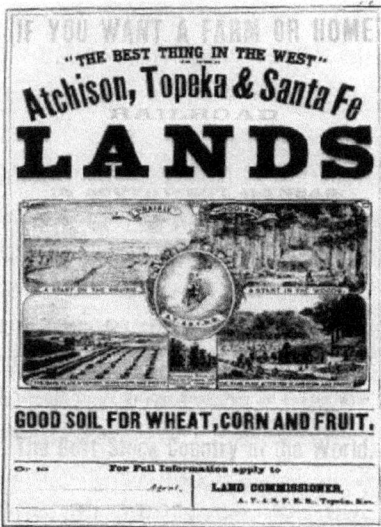

as early as the 1860's, it was during the years of 1885 thru 1910 that the majority of my ancestors left their Volga villages for other lands. While my Direct Ancestors all eventually traveled to the San Joaquin Valley (around Fresno and Visalia) in California, many of their brothers, sisters, uncles, aunts, and cousins and other relatives settled in the German areas of the states of Colorado, Idaho, Illinois, Kansas, Maryland,Michigan, Minnesota, Montana, Nebraska, New York, North Dakota, Oklahoma, Oregon, Washington, Wisconsin, and Wyoming. Volga Germans became closely associated with the sugar beet industry in Colorado and western Nebraska, others became wheat growers in the Dakotas and in Canada; some later became orchard and grape growers in California.[62] One thing that most helped the migration was the sponsorship of the railroads and their widespread advertisements.[63]

California

The history of the Volga German-Russians was thoroughly covered in a speech given by (distant Cousin) Diana Bell at the 1997 AHSGR convention. I cannot tell the story any better, so I have included it below in an edited-shortened version.

116 Years of Volga Germans in Fresno

"In the beginning, there were 10 families of Germans from Russia, who arrived in Fresno, CA on June 19, 1887. On May 8, along with 219 other immigrants, they had left the villages of Straub and Stahl am Tarlyk, on the Wiesenseite of the Volga River, journeying westward traveling by wagon, train, and boat through Poland, East Prussia, and Brandenburg to Bremen, Germany, the port of embarkation. When they docked in New York, they intended to go to Lincoln, Nebraska. 52 days later, 31 of these pioneers arrived at the old Southern Pacific Railroad Depot in Fresno, California. They brought their families to this great San Joaquin Valley to seek a better life for themselves and scouting for other families in their home villages in Russia. According to Alex C. Nilmeier, of Fresno, his grandfather Philip Nilmeier had become acquainted with a Jewish salesman on board ship. He was a man of the world who believed the San Joaquin Valley had great potential as an agricultural area. Philip Nilmeier was able to convince ten families to change their destination from Lincoln, NE to Fresno. In 1919, he said that certain articles in a little booklet, setting forth the attractions of Fresno County, for working people, also induced him to break away from the homeland.

From the village of Straub came:
John Carl Kerner, & wife - Elizabeth Rudolph Kerner and daughter, Elisa

Christian Karle, & wife - Maria Christina Wulf Kerner

Michael Karle, & wife - Christina Elizabeth Andreas Karle

Mrs. Sophia Elizabeth Metzler, and children - John August and Christine Margaret

John Conrad Metzler, & wife - Maria Christina Rudolph Metzler

John Daniel Steitz, & wife - Catherine Seifert Steitz

From the village of Stahl am Tarlyk came:
John August Berg, & wife - Catherine, and children - Maria Catherine, Peter & Henry

Philip Nilmeier, & wife - Maria Catherine & children - John Peter, Conrad & Adam

George and Philip Nilmeier

From the Steppe came:
Conrad Mehling

Jacob Mehling, & wife, and two children

In the San Joaquin Valley and Fresno, CA area, these are well known names even today. These people started the population growth of Fresno and the surrounding area by leading some 35,000 Germans from Russia to immigrate here. As reports filtered around the world, momentum reached the peak years during 1909-1920. While many thousands of Volga-Germans had migrated to the United States prior to 1887, few had reached the Pacific Coast or the San Joaquin Valley. According to John Conrad Metzler, one of the first, he and a number of the prospective settlers had been in communication with an agent, Missler by name, of the Nord-Deutsche-Lloyd Steamship Company, from Bremen, Germany, who recommended the "fertile lands" of the San Joaquin Valley of California. Whether the agent actually knew of conditions in California or merely booked the immigrants across the US for the added revenue, may never be known. The steamship line arranged for all details and made Fresno the destination.

Most of them arrived with very little in goods or money but with a willingness to work hard, to achieve a home and a living for their families by honest means. They came with the clothes on their backs, a few rubles in their pockets, a Bible, the German Wolga-Gesangbuch, Starck's Prayer Book, and a few other items of importance. Also, owing a debit to someone back in Russia for advancing the ship fare, which was about $200. Their great faith in God gave them the courage to face a strange land, unknown language, to start all over. These hardy German immigrants had but one resolve- to be independent, to own land, practice their chosen religion and to raise their families to be good citizens.

Upon arriving in Fresno, with no previous arrangements having been made, they were very lucky to be met by a Mr. Zumkeller, Mr. Green and Mr. Goldstein. These three early-day Germans operated small businesses and went out to greet them and see if they could help with lodging and work for our 10 families. Imagine their delight to be greeted by the German language in this strange land. The three men helped feed the hungry immigrants and found them lodging for the night. Mr. Goldstein had a two-story rent house for some of them to live in and helped find jobs for the men folk in the country. Philip Nilmeier started to work for him the next morning, carrying brick and hod.

From a transcript of an interview with John Conrad Metzler:

"My wife and I found lodging with a saloonkeeper who was German. On my second day in Fresno, in company with a friend, I went downtown in search of work. We were soon approached by a representative of the local water company, who made signs to us and handed us each a pick and shovel. Then, going into the street, he marked off a square and motioned for us to dig. We soon uncovered some pipes which the official examined and then told us to cover again. The idea of water being piped into homes and buildings was entirely new to us, for never had we seen anything like it in the villages of Russia. We worked all day uncovering pipes after which we returned the tools to the office and each received a silver dollar. We looked at the dollar and then remembered the pitiful wages in Russia, and we felt we had come to the right spot. All during that summer, we worked at odd jobs and earned as much as $10 to $12 dollars a week".

Another immigrant, John Carl Kerner, had been planning to leave Straub even before May of 1887. At a meeting of the community in Straub, in March, the members of the Colony gave permission for John Carl and his family, to go abroad.

Fresno County had a real estate boom going in 1887 and it may have been copies of one of the two newspapers then in existence, or one of their real state propaganda publications which reached the hands of people on the Volga, or, more probably fell to the offices of the steamship lines. The Southern Pacific Railway Company was also a strong influence in offering exceptionally low fares for immigrants and operating cars of a special type for migrating home seekers. They needed railroad workers, also.

Tragedy struck within the first month after their arrival. Many of the children were stricken with a virulent type of measles. Seven of the children died. Dr. Chester Rowell, who played an important role in the development of Fresno, became the friends of the Volga-Germans, although he had a limited knowledge of German. He took care of the funeral and burial arrangements. Due to a fire that destroyed the registry office, the families were not able to later place monuments over the graves in Potter's Field. Thus, the first Volga-German immigrants lie in nameless graves. Only 2 adults of the original band were alive in 1947, and only one remained in 1948.

Although Fresno was having a real estate boom, our Germans were poor and were unable to buy lots at this time. Work was plentiful in construction, viticulture and fruit packing. They followed the crops around, the whole family working at picking, cutting and drying apricots, then on to the peach harvest, finally came the grape harvest. While mother picked grapes, often the smallest children slept under the grapevines. The type of work was not important so long as they could make a living.

The first spare money went back to Russia to pay for their passage over; the next to buy a home of their own and eventually to buy farms. A major trait of thrift helped them to get ahead. The depression of 1893-1895 saw a decline in real estate values. Hundreds of farms were lost through foreclosures but because they were very frugal, the Germans were able to buy or lease property at deflated prices. Laborers became landowners.

The first immigrants moved into a poor section of Fresno, in the southwest part of town. Attracted by their countrymen, subsequent immigrants quite naturally gravitated to this same area. Since they were Germans from Russia, other townsmen referred to this area as "Roosian or Germantown". This area was bound by other ethnic groups; Italian, Armenian, Chinese. Regardless of how dilapidated the area you had to drive through, suddenly, south of Ventura Ave, there was a distinct change that was noticeable to even a casual observer. Homes were painted and in good repair, lawns and yards were neat and clean, driveways swept. Clean, honest and hardworking people. It was joked that if a leaf fell, they took turns rushing out to pick it up. (Some say that was their evening entertainment.)

The pattern of living in Fresno was vastly different from that of the Volga River country. Lumber was plentiful and cheap, the climate mild. As soon as land was purchased, homes were built. Usually a small frame house which was added to, as the family increased and money became available. Whether all their time was spent farming or they worked in the City and farmed out in the countryside, they came into close contact with other ethnic and native-born people.

A huge step in the direction of assimilation was taken. Most parents wanted their families to become "Americanized" and to speak English, as soon as possible. Other changes in the family life style came into being. Where the son used to bring his bride home and all lived under the same roof, within a generation, young people who desired to follow the American pattern, established homes of their own immediately after

42

marriage. While living in Russia, they kept to themselves. But here in Fresno, they learned English and became citizens of the US. The 1st & 2nd generations seldom married outside their ethnic group, but the following generations inter-married with other nationalities." [64]

Volga German-Russian California Areas [65]

"Our great country and towns were built on the sweat and labor of immigrants from many countries. Our ancestors worked very hard so that we could live in this modern world of today. From time eternal, parents have always wanted a better life for their children than they had. As with most villages or towns, Fresno was nothing much to start with. It took far sighted men to dream and invent and put into reality the means to build the San Joaquin Valley into the Bread Basket that it is.

Located in the heart of the Great Central Valley, very near the center of California, Fresno is a window into the heartland, the richest agricultural region of the state. Transformed from aridity by large scale irrigation, this water-dependent landscape has been the fastest growing region of California." [66]

Fresno was not the only California town the Volga Russian-Germans settled in. Bakersfield, Parlier, Visalia, Lodi, Loma Linda, Sanger, and others became their hometowns.[67]

Colorado

The towns of Berthoud, Brighton, Colorado Springs, Denver, Eaton, Ft. Collins, Ft. Lupton, Ft. Morgan, Globeville, Greeley,[68] Kit Carson, La Junta, Lamar, Longmont, Loveland, Moreno, Ordway, Pueblo, Rocky Ford, Sterling, Sugar City, and Windsor all had Volga German-Russians that settled them.[69]

In the early 1900s, the South Platte River Valley Great Western Sugar Company needed laborers for handwork in the sugar beet fields and in the beet sugar factories. They advertised for laborers from outside the area, and got a response from the Volga German-Russian groups. The Sugar Company's main concern was a supply of cheap labor, and with this in mind, decided on a family system of labor by securing fathers with large families of children. They assumed that women and children would also work the fields, and this is exactly what the Volga German families provided. This profited both the Sugar Company and the Volga German families. By 1928, most of the German-Russian field workers had been able to move up to tenant farming, or had saved enough money to purchase their own farms. Some had left farming and moved into homes in the towns. German-Russian communities were established in Larimer and Weld counties, in Andersonville, Buckingham Place in Fort Collins, and Ziler or Wentz near Beebe Draw in southwestern LaSalle, Windsor, Eaton and Wellington. Many of the descendants of the original Volga German-Russian sugar beet field workers still reside in the South Platte River Valley.[70]

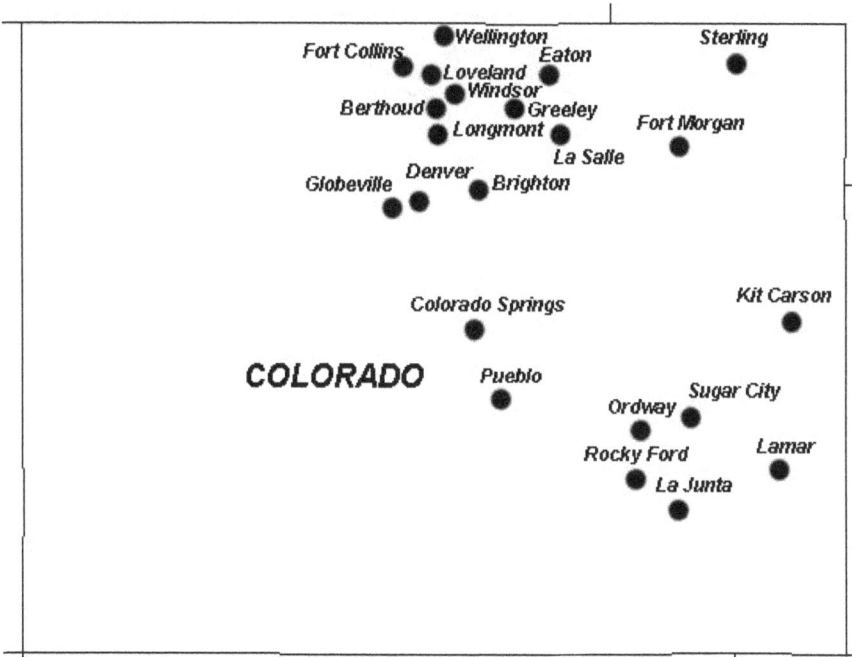

Volga German-Russian Colorado Areas [71]

Idaho

The towns of Blackfoot, Burley, Burton, Jerome, Melbeta, and Thornton; and the counties of Mindoka and Washington all had groups of Volga German-Russians that settled in them.[72] Of the more than 300,000 Volga Germans who came to the United States about 2500 settled in the Palouse country of Latha County in North Idaho.[73]

Volga German-Russian Idaho Areas [74]

Illinois

The towns of Aurora, Chicago, Dolton, Riverdale and Rockford all had groups of Volga German-Russians that settled in them.[75] In Chicago, the Volga Germans were employed as factory workers[76] and made their homes in the section of Jefferson Park and suburb of Maywood.[77]

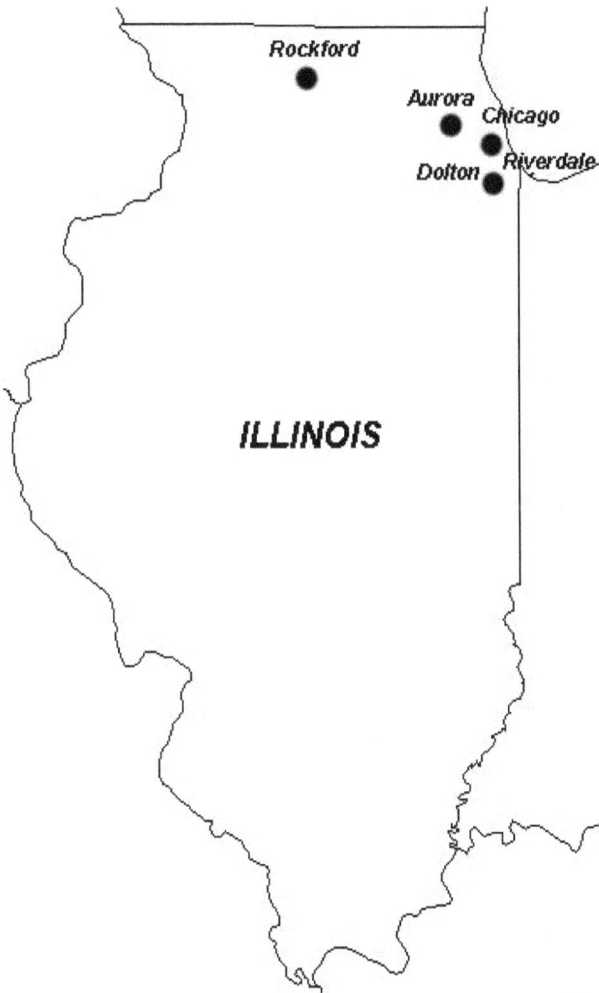

Volga German-Russian Illinois Areas [78]

Iowa

The towns of Fort Dodge and Red Oak both had groups of Volga German-Russians that settled in them.[79]

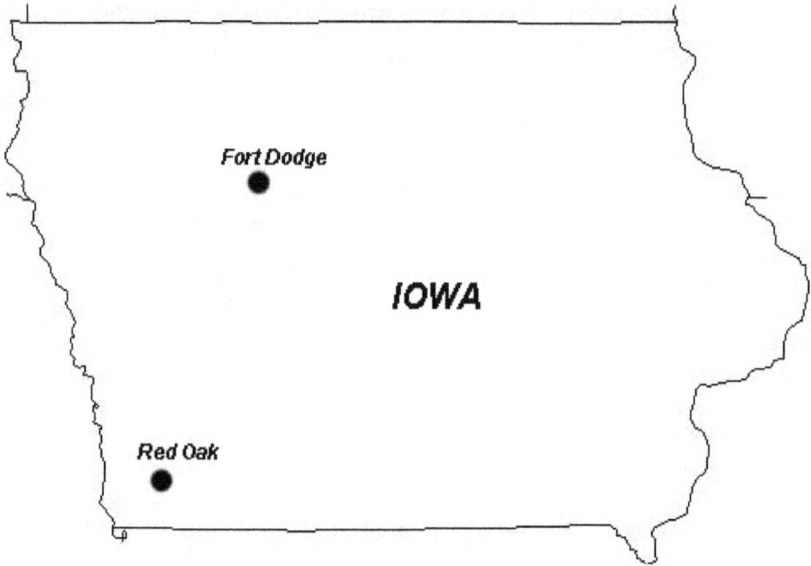

Fort Dodge
●

IOWA

Red Oak
●

Volga German-Russian Iowa Areas [80]

Kansas

The towns of Albert, Alexander, Antonino, Bison, Bunkerhill, Catherine, Durham, Ellsworth, Galatia, Great Bend, Hayes, Herrington, Herzog, Hoisington, LaCrosse, Liebenthal, Lincolnville, Loretta, Lydia, Marienthal, McCracken, Medicine Lodge, Milberger, Munjor, Nashville, Oakley, Olmitz, Otis, Pawnee Rock, Pfeifer, Russell, Salina, Schoenchen, St.Peter, Susank, Topeka, and Victoria

all had groups of Volga German-Russians that settled in them.[81]

The Volga Germans of Roman Catholic, Lutheran, and Baptist denominations originally settled mainly in the areas of Ellis, Russell, and Rush counties in Kansas.

The five men shown in the picture[82] were elected by some of the German settlers along the Volga River to act as scouts to investigate the land around Nebraska. They were Peter Leiker (of Obermunjou), Peter Stecklein (of Zug), Anton Wasinger (of Schoenchen), Nicholas Schamne (of Graf), and Jacob Ritter (of Luzern). They left Obermunjou, Russia in 1874, and eventually returned to the Volga area with a favorable report. From this, many Colonists would emigrate in 1875, but settle in Ellis County, Kansas.[83]

Left to Right:
Peter Stecklein, Jacob Ritter, Nicholas Schamne, Peter Leiker, and Anton Wasinger

The first Volga German group left Katharinenstadt in October 1875. First Bremen, then Baltimore, and eventually they arrived in Topeka less than sixty days later on November 28. The families settled temporarily in North Topeka while their leaders searched for suitable lands to live on. They first went with C. B. Schmidt to inspect Santa Fe Railroad lands near Great Bend. The price at $5.00 an acre was too much. With the help of Adam Roedelheimer and Martin Allen, they were able to look to at the lands of the Kansas Pacific Railroad in Ellis County.[84]

Even in Ellis County, many homesteaded the land instead of purchasing from the railroad because of the land price.[85] The first families arrived in Hays and Victoria Settlement in February 1876.[86] These first settlers rented a building at the corner of 13th & Fort. Each day, they drove their wagons to the present site of Catherine and built their houses. Upon finishing their homes, the entire group moved together and formally established Catherine on April 8, 1876. [87]

Another group had established Liebenthal. This is the oldest of the villages and the only one situated in Rush County. Located on Big Timber Creek, the original founders were among the large group that left Saratov, Russia October 24, 1875. [88]

Herzog (Victoria) became the largest and most important of the Volga German colonies in Ellis County. Also established on April 8, 1876, most of the early settlers were farmers and peasants. The religious dedication of the early settlers is regarded nationally with profound respect of the unbelievable accomplishment associated with the construction of "The Cathedral of the Plains." Herzog was incorporated in 1913, gave up the Herzog name, and took the name Victoria after Queen Victoria of England.[89]

The settlement of Pfeifer is about 10 miles south of Victoria on the south bank of the Smoky Hill River. The settlers date of arrival not exact, but it was around August 21 or 24, 1876. More Volga Germans arrived in Pfeifer in October and November 1877. Pfeifer was like the other Volga German communities in Ellis County. The settlers endured crop failures, major depressions and poverty. [90]

Munjor was founded as part of the largest single expedition to emigrate from Russia. On July 8, 1876, 108 families left Saratov and arrived in Herzog in August 1876. They stayed in Herzog for a few weeks and then moved to the present site of Munjor.[91]

Other groups followed arriving during the spring and summer, especially in August. By the end of 1876, about 1,200 Roman Catholic Faith Volga Germans had moved to Ellis and Rush counties, and another group of Lutheran Faith had settled along Landon creek in Russell County.[92] Schoenchen was established in 1877, and was created by spin-off from an original because of conflict among the first settlers.[93] After 1877, large immigrant parties of German-Russians from the Volga region became common. By this time, many were settling and finding homes in a large number of counties of central and western Kansas. The total number of German-Russian immigrants into Kansas in the 1870's was estimated at about 12,000.

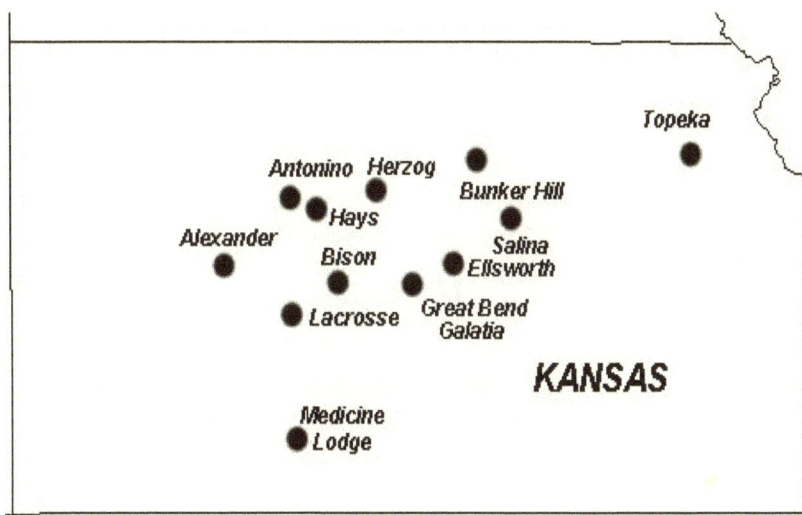

Volga German-Russian Kansas Areas [94]

Maryland

One of the entry ports into the United States was Baltimore. While most emigrants kept going, the city of Baltimore did have groups of Volga German-Russians that stayed on and settled in it.[95]

Volga German-Russian Maryland Areas [96]

Michigan

The towns of Applegate, AuGres, Bay City, Barren Springs, Brimley, Deckerville, Flint, Glencoe, Mayville, McGregor, Peck, Port Huron, Reese, Saginaw, Sault Ste. Marie, Sebewaing, Swartz, Swartz Creek, and Thumb Area all had groups of Volga German-Russians that settled in them.[97] Volga German-Russian settlers arrived in the Thumb area of Michigan around 1911. They probably came to the area for work in the sugar beet industry that was flourishing at the time. Since they had grown sugar beets back in the Volga area, they were experienced. They found immediate employment, and whole families worked in the fields thinning, blocking and harvesting the beets.[98]

Volga German-Russian Michigan Areas [99]

Minnesota

The towns of Glencoe, Mountain Lake, and St. Paul all had groups of Volga German-Russians that settled in them.[100]

MINNESOTA

Glencoe

St Paul

Mountain Lake

Volga German-Russian Minnesota Areas [101]

Montana

The towns of Billings, Edgar, Hardin, Huntley, Laurel, Missoula, Park City, and Worden all had groups of Volga German-Russians that settled in them.[102] Many of the Volga Germans earned a living working in the beet fields near Laurel and Billings. At first, they lived in Lincoln, Nebraska in the winter, and then in the spring, they would board up their houses and travel to the Montana beet fields. Eventually, many of them permanently settled around Laurel and Billings.[103]

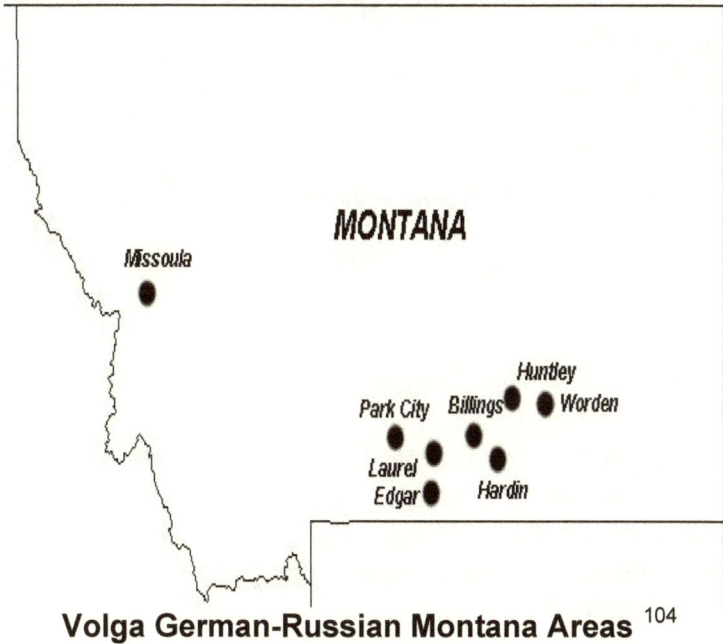

Volga German-Russian Montana Areas [104]

Nebraska

The towns of Bayard, Campbell, Culbertson, Fairmont, Friend, Gering, Harvard, Hastings, Henderson, Lincoln, Linwood, Lyman, McCook, McGrew, Minatare, Mitchell, Morrill, Scottsbluff, Sutton, Valentine, and York all had groups of Volga German-Russians that settled in them.[105]

Volga German-Russian Nebraska Areas [106]

In Lincoln, Nebraska, the Volga Germans typically lived on the north side and the south side. In the spring, they would board up their homes and travel to the beet fields by train. In the fall, they would return with their earnings to spend the winter in Lincoln. [107]

On July 22, 1876, a small group of Volga German-Russians from the colony of Kolb set sail for the United States via Bremen, Germany. Supposedly, this group was directed to the state of Wisconsin, but they did not like all the forests of Wisconsin. In August 1876, they found had made their way to Hastings, Adams County, Nebraska. The group stayed in Hastings for a while, and then moved on to Campbell, Franklin County, Nebraska by the fall of 1876. There they built a "settlement house." Their first homes were simple dugouts in the ground. For the first few years, the group at Campbell was quite mobile with part of the group also living on homesteads in Hitchcock County, Nebraska.[108]

New Jersey

The city of town Newark had a group of Volga German-Russians that settled in it. [109]

Volga German-Russian New Jersey Area [110]

New York

Pine Island, New York was a small and isolated enclave of German-Russians from the Volga Colony of Yagodnaya, where they raised onions or became dairy farmers.[111] Stuyvesant Falls also had a German-Russian population.

Volga German-Russian New York Areas [112]

North Dakota

The towns of Alsen, Donhoff, Elliott, Lisbon, Munch, and Shields all had groups of Volga German-Russians that settled in them.[113]

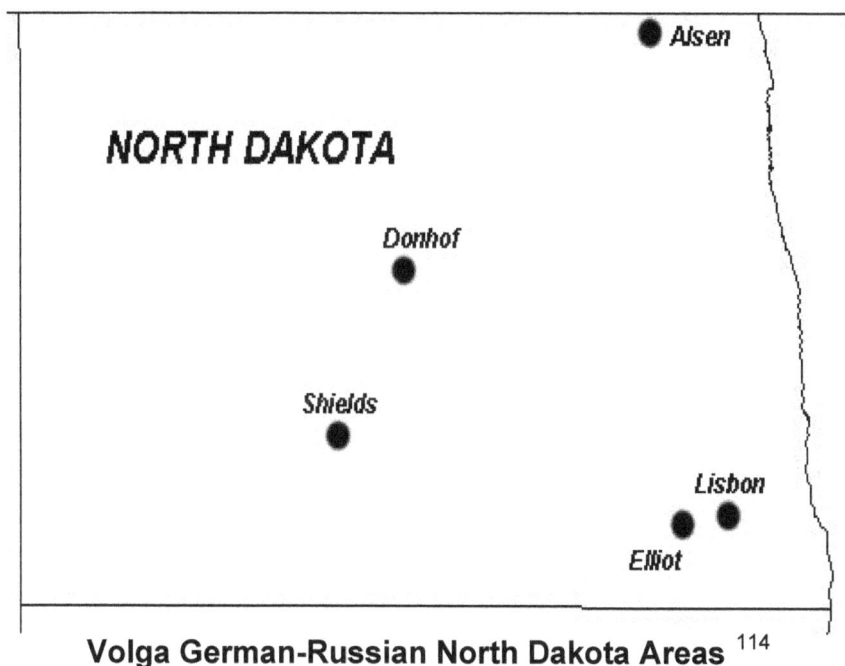

Volga German-Russian North Dakota Areas [114]

Ohio

The town of Wauseon had a group of Volga German-Russians that settled in it.[115]

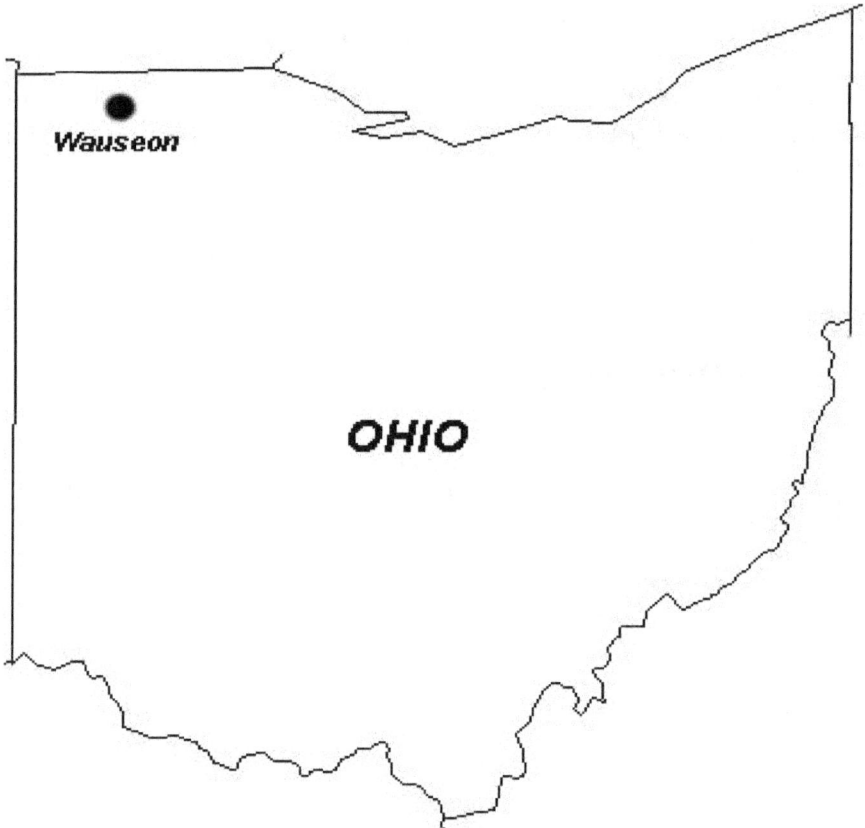

Volga German-Russian Ohio Area [116]

Oklahoma

The towns of Alva, Bessie, Hitchcock, Mangum, Moore, Okeene, Shattuck, and Woodward, and the Panhandle area all had groups of Volga German-Russians that settled in them.[117] Some Volga Germans landed up in Enid, Oklahoma for work in the fields. Over time, as families grew smaller with fewer children, work in the beet fields became unprofitable, and they branched out and learned trades.[118]

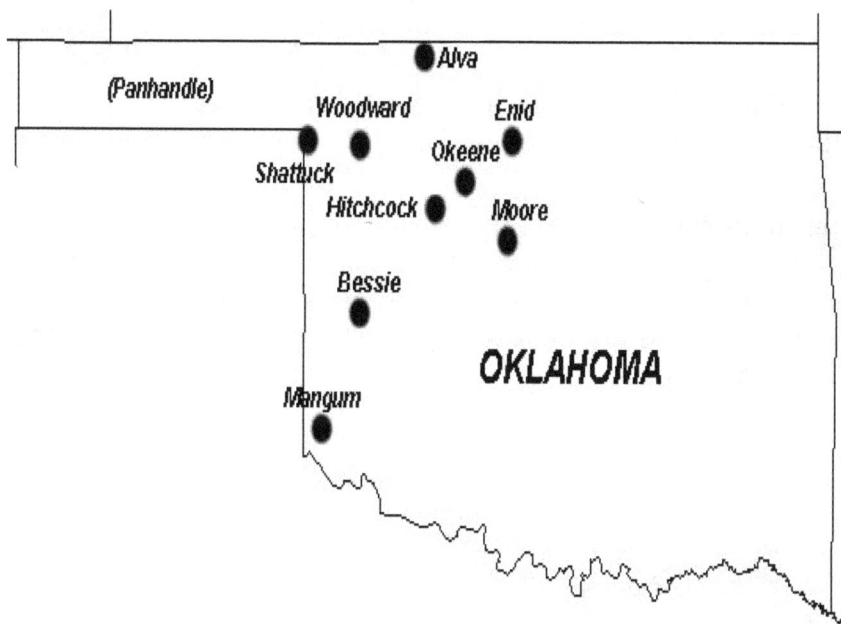

Volga German-Russian Oklahoma Areas [119]

Oregon

The towns of Portland and Salem both had groups of Volga German-Russians that settled in them.[120] Portland is the oldest settlement of Evangelical Volga Germans in Oregon. It was established in 1882 when colonists from the Volga Colony of Norka, who had at first settled in Iowa and Nebraska, came by train to San Francisco.

These Volga Germans worked for the Union Pacific Railroad [121] after starting in Nebraska.[122] They landed up in San Francisco, and then sailed to Portland where they found jobs as day laborers in the factories [123] and settled in Portland's east side "Little Russia." [124] Another group of Volga Germans had left Iowa for Walla Walla, Washington, but after spending three months in Walla Walla, had moved on to Portland as early as 1882.[125] For about six years, there were no new arrivals, but from 1888 to 1890, Portland became home to groups of Volga German colonists from the colonies of Balzer and Frank. The great majority of German-Russians came to Portland between the years 1890-1905.

German-Russians from the Volga Colony of Alt-Norka made up the majority of around 500 families in the settlement, and populated an entire ward in northeast Portland.[126] Former neighbors once again lived and worked side by side, as they did in Alt-Norka.

Volga German-Russian Oregon Areas [127]

This Old World village stretched along Northeast Union and Seventh avenues from Fremont to Shaver. Just as in the old Volga Colonies, you could see women wearing brown woolen shawls and headscarves, and overhear them talking with Hessian accents.[128]

South Dakota

The town of Yankton had Volga German-Russians that settled in it.[129]

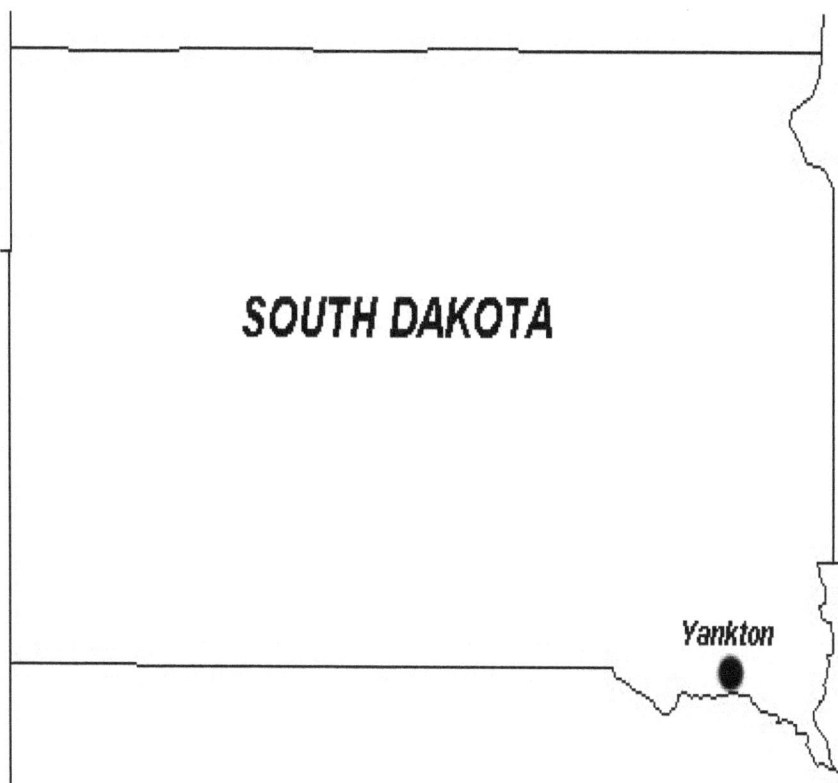

Volga German-Russian South Dakota Area [130]

Texas

The Lipscomb County area had Volga German-Russians that settled in it.[131]

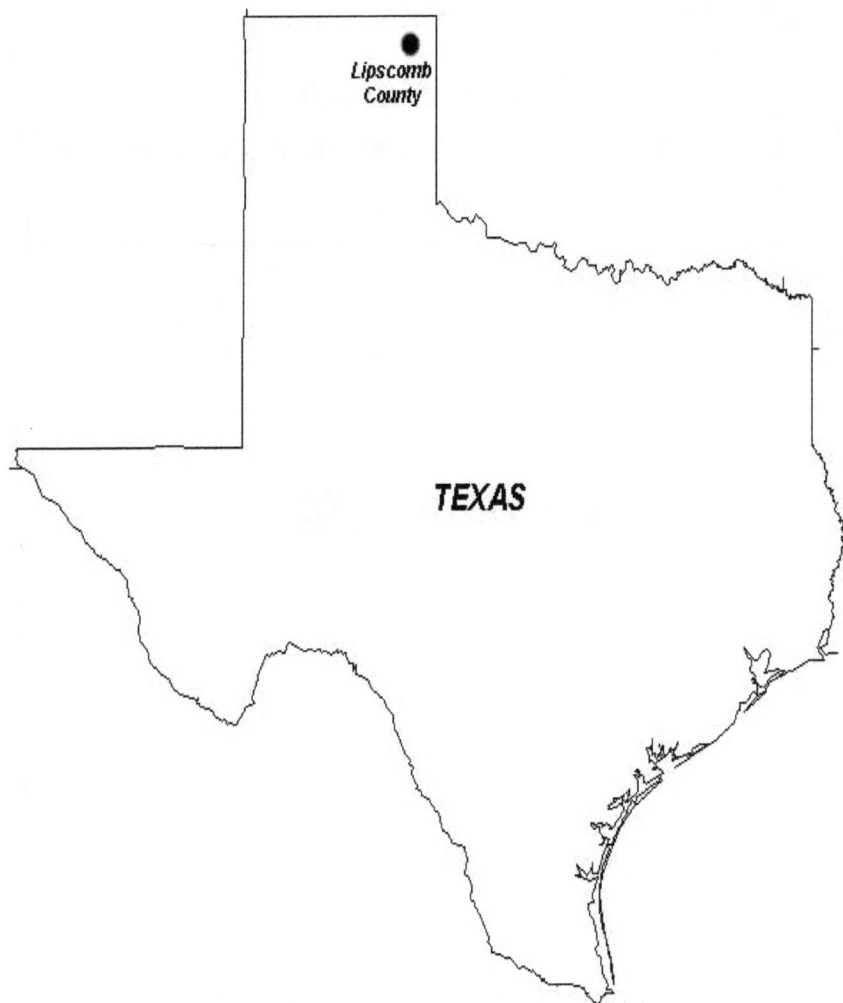

Lipscomb
County

TEXAS

Volga German-Russian Texas Area [132]

Washington

The towns of Bellingham, Bickleton, Bremerton, Colfax, Endicott, Farmer, Longview, Moses Lake, Odessa, Ritzville, Spokane, Sunnyside, Tacoma, Toppenish, Walla Walla, and Yakima all had groups of Volga German-Russians that settled in them.[133] Originally, some of the Volga Germans set up farms in Nebraska and Kansas, but unfavorable climate and farming conditions made them to look elsewhere for better farming conditions. They became some of the earliest German American settlers in the Pacific Northwest. Their numbers multiplied starting in the early 1880s when they were guided to the Pacific Northwest by aggressive railroad company advertisement.

Volga German-Russian Washington Areas [134]

Companies such as the Northern Pacific Railroad needed unskilled labor to help develop the area. They also wanted to sell the lands they had received from the US Government. The railroads hired agents in the East, Midwest, and in Europe. They also advertised the area extensively in newspapers, distributed thousands of circulars "pushing" the wonderful Pacific Northwest, and offered cheap fares and employment to lure immigrants to the area.[135]

Wisconsin

The towns of Chilton, Fond du Lac, Milwaukee, Oshkosh, Racine, and Sheboygan all had groups of Volga German-Russians that settled in them.[136]

In response to a woodworkers strike, the Paine Lumber Company located in Oshkosh actively recruited Volga Germans from Russia to be replacement workers.[137] Paine's lumber advertised employment to new immigrants and inexpensive company apartments. The first few families came to Oshkosh from the Volga Colony of Yagodnaya in 1899.[138] They were Lutheran and built Christ Lutheran Church and Zion Lutheran Church, and settled on the Oshkosh West Side along Sawyer St. [139]

By 1900, one-third of the Oshkosh population was German.[140] In 1901, a flood of immigrants followed. The West Side quickly became a new Yagodnaya neighborhood allowing the tight knit community to stay together. Oshkosh became one of the largest settlements of people from the colony. Eventually, some became unhappy with factory work and left the jobs at Paine Lumber to try their hand at farming in other areas. Some were successful; some were not and returned to the factory jobs in Oshkosh.[141]

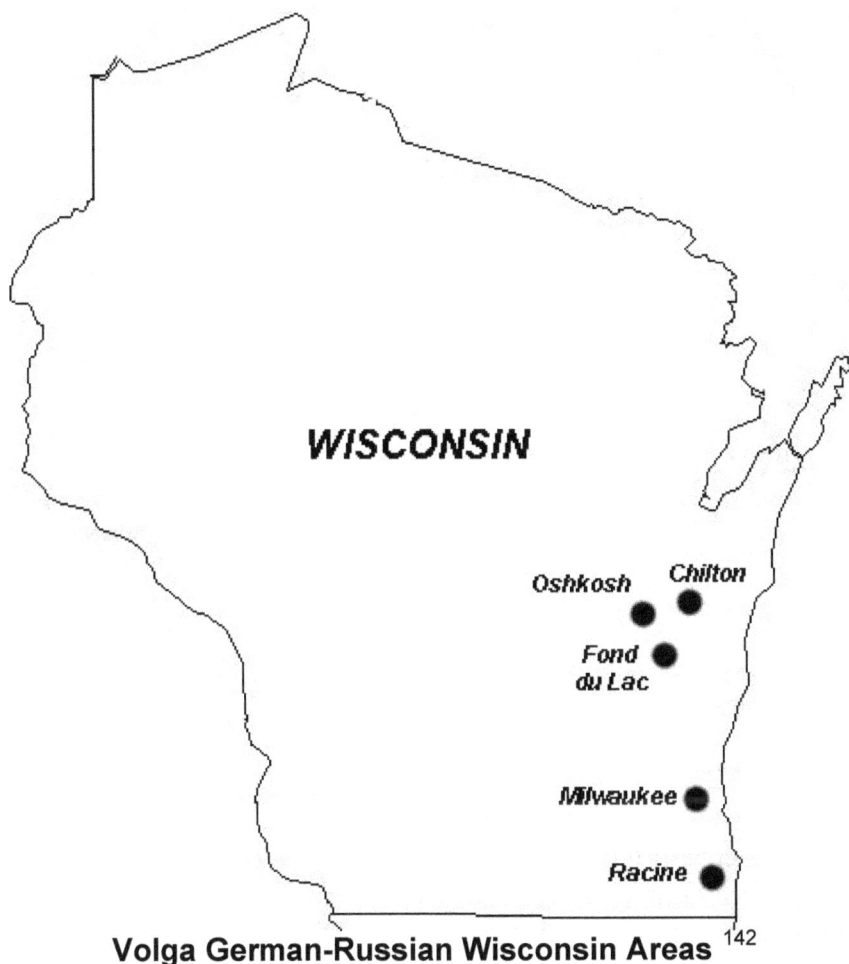

WISCONSIN

Oshkosh · Chilton

Fond du Lac ·

Milwaukee ·

Racine ·

Volga German-Russian Wisconsin Areas [142]

Wyoming

The towns of Casper, Cheyenne, Hawk Springs, Lander, Lingle, Lovell, Powell, Riverton, Sheridan, Torrington, Wheatland, and Worland all had groups of Volga German-Russians that settled in them. [143]

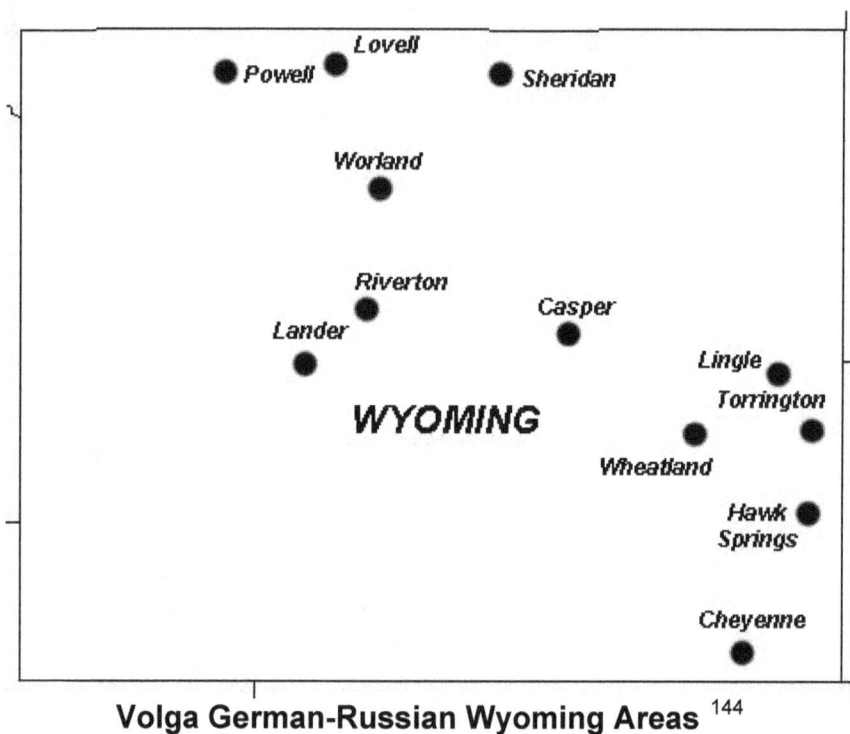

Volga German-Russian Wyoming Areas [144]

Alberta, Canada

Volga German-Russians from the villages of Dreispitz, Huck, Norka, Pobochnoye, Shcherbakovka, and Jagodnaya Polyana immigrated to Alberta beginning in 1892. They settled in the Calgary area, and west of Edmonton in Stony Plain and Glory Hills. Both these areas attracted many more settlers from the Volga in the following years near Trochu, Beiseker and Duffield. Reformed Faith Volga German-Russians also settled in 1897 near Mellowdale in the Barrhead area. [145]

Saskatchewan, Canada

In 1887, Volga German-Russians immigrated to Canada and established a settlement north of Yorkton near Rhein in

Saskatchewan.[146] Other colonists from Schuck, Holstein, Bangert, Warenburg, Grimm, Ahrenfeld, Kratzke, Kolb, Vollmer, Holstein, Hussenbach, and Rosenberg settled in Denzil, Duvall, Flowering Well, Flowing Well, Hodgeville, Jansen, Kerrobert, Lanigan, Luseland, Macklin, Morse, Regina, and Wadena.[147]

Volga German-Russian Areas [148]

Manitoba, Canada

Volga German-Russians from Bangert, Stahl am Tarlyk, Balzer, Galka, Holstein, Hussenbach, Kamyshin, Rosenberg, Unterdorf, and Warenburg immigrated to Canada and established settlements in Winnipeg, Gladstone, and Lydiatt.[149]

Russia

Some of the Volga German-Russians left and moved to other areas of Russia such as Ziskaukasia, the Don Region and other southern provinces, to the Ural, West Siberia and Central Asia. New German settlements quickly sprang up.[150]

Chapter 4
Emigration in around 1900

Moving and traveling in the late 1800's and early 1900's was unlike anything we do today. This was still the time of the horse and cart, and the Railroad was the modern conveyance. Automobiles and trucks had not arrived yet. To say that a move of any kind would be difficult is an understatement. Yet, the Volga German-Russians packed up their valuables (as their ancestors did 135 years earlier) and set out for a new land.

The following is a description of what my Great Grandfather and Mother (Philip Kaiser and Maria Katharina Simon) went through to get from Warenburg, Russia to Fresno, California (from my book "*Origins and Ancestors Families Karle & Kaiser of the German-Russian Volga Colonies.*"

"Philip married Maria Katharina (Katie) Simon, daughter of Johann Conrad (Red) Simon and Maria Christina Krämer on January 25, 1905 in Warenburg, Privalnjoe, Samara, Russia. They had a son, Henry, born October 24, 1905; and a daughter, Anna, born February 06, 1907. The left photo below is Philip; the right is wife Katie Simon (both 1910). [151]

It would appear that family patriarch Johann Conrad (Red) Simon made the decision to move his extended family to the United States. What the reasons for emigration

were, no one really knows. However, Philip's son (my father) told me that his father said that he left to keep from having to join the Russian Navy.[152] In any case, once the decision was made, Philip must have supported his father-in-law. Johann Conrad (Red) Simon was first to emigrate, followed some months later by Philip. He probably began his emigration from Russia to the United States by getting tickets and a passport. The tickets could be obtained through the F. Missler Travel Agency in Bremen, Germany, an agency that specialized in helping German-Russians travel to America. Tickets cost around $200 or 400 Russian Rubles. A Passport cost around $6.00 or 12 Rubles.

With the ticket and passport, he probably traveled north by train from Warenburg to Saratov, west through the cities of Smolensk and Vitebsk, Russia to Libau, Latvia, and then by ship to Bremen, Germany.[153] There, he boarded the ship "Estonia"[154] (formerly the ship "Yorkshire"). Philip arrived in the United States on August 29, 1907 through Ellis Island (Manifest #25).

From New York immigration records, we know that at age 21 he was about 69" tall, dark complexion with brown eyes and "fair" color hair. The records also tell us that he listed his wife, Maria Katherine (Katie) Simon, as his Point of Contact back in

S.S. ESTONIA

Warenburg, Russia. From New York, Philip was on his way to the address of Johann Conrad (Red) Simon (his father-in law) at 309 E Street in Fresno, California.

His wife, Katie (as she was called) and their two children, Henry and Anna, sailed for the United States from Libau,

S.S. LITUANIA

Latvia with her brother, John Jacob Simon, on the ship "Lituania"[155] and arrived March 5, 1908 at Ellis Island (Manifest #s 18-20).

From New York immigration records, we know that at age 24, Katie was about 62" tall, dark complexion with brown eyes and brown hair. After a railroad trip across the United States, she and her two children joined her husband in Visalia, Tulare County, California. Visalia, which is south of Fresno, is where her husband and her father, Johann Conrad (Red) Simon had settled in 1907." [156]

Hundreds of thousands of Volga German-Russians made the same journey as my Grandparents. Each of their stories is unique, but so much of each story follows the same path.

The Entry Ports

When you think of where your ancestor entered in to the United States, your first thought is probably .... Statue of Liberty and Ellis island.You might be right, but you might be wrong.

Determining which port is the correct one may require you to search the records of possible several ports. One of the problems is that most passenger lists were handwritten by each arriving Ship Offficer. Deciphering this handwriting was often difficult (and wrong) when the lists were later indexed.

The five major U.S. arrival ports for the United States in the 1800's and 1900's New York, Boston, Baltimore, Philadelphia and New Orleans.

Other less frequently used ports were Savannah, Georgia; Gloucester, Massachusetts; Gulfport and Pascagoula, Mississippi; Charleston, South Carolina; and Galveston, Texas.[157] There were even more depending on the entry year.

New York (Castle Garden, Barge Office and Ellis Island) was the most commonly used port. Before August 1855, there really was not a dedicated immigration processing center in the New York harbor. Lost and confused immigrants were at risk from the criminals that prowled the open wharves with only one goal; to take advantage of gullible newcomers and separate them from their property and money.[158]

Castle Garden around 1900 [159]

On August 3, 1855, Castle Garden was opened on a small island off the southwest tip of Manhattan. New York State operated Castle Garden (part of Castle Clinton) through 18 April, 1890 as the first immigrant examining and processing center. Between 1855 and 1889, more than eight million immigrants -- two out of every three persons immigrating to the United States in this period -- passed through the Garden. [160]

The Immigration Act of 1882 (Owen Law), which authorized the Treasury Secretary to contract with the states for enforcement of that law, gave control of immigration to the Federal Government. [161] On April 1, 1890, the Treasury Secretary terminated the immigration contract with New York State. On April 18, 1890, Treasury assumed total control of immigration at the Port of New York. The New York State authorities were not happy with this development, and refused to allow the federal government to use the existing Castle Garden examining and processing center. [162]

Acting quickly the next day, the Federal Government established a temporary center in the old Barge Office at the foot of Whitehall Street near the Battery at the southeast end of Manhattan.

When Immigration was in the hands of New York State, relatively few immigrants were refused entry. Under the old law during the period from January 1 to April 18, 1890, a total of 85,952 immigrants arrived at the port of New York, and only 82 (less than 0.1% were sent back to their original country. Under the new law and Federal control, about five times that number were denied entry. [163]

The first Ellis Island immigrant examining and processing center opened on January 1, 1892. The original Ellis Island Immigrant Station was built of wood and slate and is not the more familiar brick structure shown in most photographs.

Ellis Island Immigrant Station around 1892 [164]

As with most wooden structures at that time, it caught on fire. On June 13, 1897 the Ellis Island immigrant examining and processing center burned to the ground along with all of the administrative records for Castle Garden for 1855-1890 and most of the records for the Barge Office.

This was in spite of the fact that the Ellis Island's entire collection of state and federal lists were stored in a underground vault. Unfortunately, the vault and its contents were also completely destroyed. [165]

Luckily, copies of the passenger lists were kept by the Customs Collector, and lists were filed in Washington, DC.

However, the Customs lists did not have as much information about passengers as did the Immigration lists. [166]

Old Barge Office about 1900 [167]

The Barge Office immigrant examining and processing center was reactivated and used from June 14, 1897 through December 16, 1900. [168]

The Ellis Island Immigration Station was rebuilt and reopened on December 17, 1900, and immigrants came through Ellis Island until 1924. [169]

Ellis Island around 1905 [170]

The Ellis Island Process

After their Atlantic Ocean ship voyage, the emigrants were exhausted and overwhelmed from their long journey, and ready for land. They probably thought they had faced the worst.

Immigrants on Atlantic Ship (packed like Sardines) [171]

As they arrived in the Ellis Island Great Hall they were immediately directed through inspections that would ensure that were disease-free and able to earn a living in the United States. [172]

Awaiting Inspections [173]

The Ellis Island Inspectors examined each of them for any sign of sickness. Those found with suspicious symptoms were separated and detained for a further more detailed inspection. The Inspectors also asked them questions as to their origins, their past, how much money they had, where they were going, and about their future plans in the United States. [174]

Some were held for failing the questions, and had to have relatives come to claim them. Those that could not satisfy the requirements were turned back. Families were sometimes had to decide on the spot whether to split up with those accepted going on, or for the whole family going back with those that were denied access. [175]

If they passed the inspections, the immigrants collected their baggage and exchanged their money for U.S. currency. For those heading to new homes in the West, a railroad agent was there to sell them tickets for the next stage of their journey. [176]

Ellis Island Inspections [177]

Baltimore

The port of Baltimore was designated as the port of entry for the North German Lloyd Line. Their first ship, the *Baltimore*, arrived in there in 1868. This shipping line carried hundreds of thousands of Germans from the northern German port of Bremen to the United States by way of Baltimore until the beginning of World War I.

The Lloyd Line brought more German immigrants into the United States through Baltimore than any other port city to include New York. Because of this, Baltimore was second only to New York as the busiest immigrant port of entry. By 1870, more than half of the Baltimore immigrant population had come from Germany, and by 1890, over one-third of the city's population spoke German.[178] Most of the Volga German-Russians that came through Baltimore on their way west did so in the late 1800's and early 1900's.

Galveston

The Port of Galveston became a port of entry beginning in 1847. Emigrants from Germany came through Galveston to Houston and then to lands west of San Antonio and north of Waco, founding towns like New Braunfels, Schulenburg and Shiner. Years later in the late 1800's and early 1900's, Volga German-Russians came through the Port of Galveston and followed the earlier Germans' path.[179]

The following is a description of what an emigrant family went through as they left Bremen, Germany and entered the United States through the Port of Galveston. While the family was Czech, and not German-Russian, their experiences were typical of all the emigrants.

"THE DIARY OF JOSEPH MARECEK
Forward
This diary was translated from the Czech language by Mrs. Anne Marecek Urban and her daughter Nancy Urban Brosig. This was done in 1979, some sixty years after it was originally written. The diary was then submitted to the book, History of Ethnic Cultures in the Ballinger Area.

THE DIARY

On the ship, Koln, we sat on July 12, 1906, and then sailed from Bremen, Germany at 4:00 a.m. on July 13, 1906.

July 13, 1906

The ocean is nice and everything is so beautiful that you can't even write about it. At 12:00 noon, the wind was real strong, and you had to be well dressed so that you wouldn't get cold. The ship waved and shook. It was a real storm, and if the ship would turn over, about 1200 people would be drowned. Everyone was getting sick. At 4:00 p.m., the ocean was calm again like a mirror. The ship went smoothly until 4:00 a.m. For 3 hours, storm so strong, that the ship rocked like a rocker. The people couldn't stand up. Everybody is seasick. My wife and 3 oldest children were lying sick as if they were dead. The 2 others, Anne and Libby, and I didn't get sick yet. At 7:00 the sea was calmer. Everyone was not so seasick, and the sea was quiet.

July 14, 15, and 16, 1906

Our ship, the Koln, came close to the English shore. We could see England from early a.m. to 7:00 p.m. First, we saw sand and land, and then forest, and the huge hills and then saw some towns. Saw so many ships, that they couldn't even be counted.

15th

Windy again. The waves were meeting us; the wind coming toward us. It was so strong, it whistled. It was awful, everybody thought they were going to drown any minute. It was so bad, that it was hard to describe and put into writing. The waves were so high the ship was nearly standing on end and then it rolled to the side until it felt like everyone was going to fall out. Everyone was rushing to the opposite side. The waves were going over the top of the ship.

July 17, 1906

Weather is pretty. Ship is going like a "doll". For how long, I don't know. Last night we saw big schools of fish. The ship didn't even once shake. I bought a Bewmen accordian. I gave 10 Rubles. Last night, I played 'till 12:00 midnight and the people danced. They have their own band. Nearly each night they have drum, piccolo, and accordian. I started playing myself and then all the band went to dance too. I play with them each night that they play.

July 18, 1906

In the a.m. it rained; pretty, ship goes quietly. For dinner we had rice pudding, 2 meats, rolls and gravy. Then everybody got seasick all over again. There are 5 or 6 American farmers who were Czech who are going with us. Also, Moravians and Germans. Weather after dinner was kind of foggy.

July 19, 1906

Foggy; lasted all night. So thick that we had not seen anything like it yet. During the day, it kind of disappeared. Then so thick that we couldn't see but about 100 steps into the ocean. Ocean is quiet. My wife, Anna, is up again on her feet.

July 20, 1906

Seas again rough. Ship is rocking more. My wife, Anna, is well. The fog is thin. Afternoon; fog gone. Sea is quiet like a "mirror". All on ship are Polish, German, Romanian, Moravian, Slovak. 1200 people on ship. Afternoon: 5:00, fog lasted 'till morning. It was so thick you couldn't see anything.

July 21, 1906
Beautiful sunshine! It is windy, it's cool, cool until noon. After dinner, beautiful and warm.

July 22, 1906 Sunday Morning
Thick fog, cold until night. At night, rains 'till half the night.

July 23, 1906
Fog, quiet ocean. Everybody is complaining about bad food. After supper the people were going to break thing up, so they were promised better food. We were being treated worse than hogs.

July 24, 1906
Food no better. Bread is raw. Sugar sold for 1 Mark. Bitter tea. "If you didn't have a good stomach , the hungry would die like dogs." Afternoon: strong wind and big waves. We were used to sugar, and although the sugar was 1 Mark for a quart, we had to buy it to keep alive.

July 25, 1906
Big waves and strong winds. Waves over the ship all night. Morning it was beautiful weather. We would be in the canal all night. For about 8 hours we could see Baltimore.

July 26, 1906
Everything is so beautiful as we were traveling through the land on each side. One didn't know on which side to look so that you could see the most. Everything is so beautiful that the eyes couldn't absorb all that God made. Can't even write how beautiful it was. The ship went around Boston; saw huge factories, homes, and buildings. Going 1 ½ hours beautiful can't even write it. Factories couldn't see over them. Most beautiful part,

were the lights at night on the shore. We could see Boston from 10:00 a.m. 'til noon ships along shore were unloading stuff. We went on to Baltimore.

July 27, 1906

Unloading barrels so many couldn't even think to count them. Even had conveyor belts to keep the barrels moving so that they wouldn't have to be carried or lifted. About 100 men were workers. Down off the ship we couldn't go. Americans could come on the ship and sell pears, bananas, and apples for 10 cents a pound. Sausage 3 pounds for 25 cents. Unloading ship all day and unloaded it all night.

July 28, 1906

After breakfast, we are playing cards, then had dinner, and then cards again. They were loading coal all night and all day. The ripples on the water were like our lakes at home. Ships all over. Baltimore each day it is interesting on water. One or two ships each day. They go around our ship. You can hear music and see dancing. Two weeks since we left home.

July 29, 1906 Sunday 6:00 a.m.

Leaving Baltimore and going back through same canal to Galveston, Texas. The same Captain of the ship was still with us (Anthony Kocemom). We sailed until 7:00 p.m. We had a good dinner like we hadn't had on ship before. Pork, potatoes and gravy, rice pudding, and sweet rolls with raisins.

July 30, 1906

Windy and ship is rocking. After breakfast, real strong wind and it was warm. At night the shores disappeared and again we have the trip from Baltimore to Galveston (1558 miles). Afternoon, strong fog, so thick, that one's shadow couldn't be seen if on deck. This lasted 'till 5:00 p.m. It left and at night pretty weather. My wife (Anna Marecek) got up.

July 31, 1906

Sea is calm and the ship "went like a doll". The people are happy and my wife is well again. The eats and food as bad as they had it before. Often, we get rotten meat. Today, we didn't even get dinner. It was so bad, you can't even write it.

August 1, 1906

This is the calmest the ocean has ever been since we left. The only waves are what our ship make. Went by small islands. Food is not for the people, but for dogs. Bad food.

August 2, 1906

Water is still calm. We went all night until 7:00 a.m. around land of Florida. It is awful hot. So hot, it is hard to believe. We spread a sheet over our heads so that the sun wouldn't be so hot while we were on deck. The night is beautiful. It is full moon. It looks like a million stars reflect in the waters. Anne (our daughter) got sick.

August 3, 1906

Seas calm and quiet. We had a little shower. It cooled things off. Anne (our daughter) got strong fever and cold. She is so hot that she is like a hot iron and has a strong cough. After dinner, we saw a "school of fish". About eight different kinds. The food was terrible. Those who don't have money can't buy a glass of beer. (Those suffer a lot). A glass of beer is 7 cents.

August 4, 1906
The water is like a "mirror". Nothing new, only that 2 men robbed something and they were told that they wouldn't let them off in America. Then they were given a beating. After dinner, we are coming into Galveston. Galveston was so much prettier than in BaltimoreThe houses along the shore. Don't know what's what because it was getting too dark. From the mainland to Galveston, a railroad track was being built.

August 5, 1906
In the morning we had to go through customs. When it was our time to go I was pleading. They wanted me to go and my family to go back to the ship, since Anne (our daughter) has smallpox. They finally let us all go back to the ship. Becannovi (the people that we traveled with) had to go on the ship with us. He was real mad and cussing us out.

August 6, 1906
About 10:00 a.m., we again came before customs. They then sent my wife (Anna) and daughters Libby and Anne to the hospital in Galveston. I took the 3 other children (Mary , Joe, and Laddie) and we went to a rooming house. To the hospital I had 15 vest. Becana were free to go and they immediately went to Rowena on a farm.

August 7, 1906
I went to the hospital with my children to see my wife and daughters, but we were not turned in. So that we would not get smallpox. It didn't cost us anything. The ship's insurance paid for all the hospital expenses. The town in beginning to grow. The streets aren't paved (a hurricane destroyed the town in 1900). A few houses are brick, most are lumber. We will be here about 3 more days because my wife and daughters are still in the hospital.

August 8 and 9, 1906

Nothing new, it is raining for 6 hours. The flowers are in bloom. Some streets were paved but the rest were sand. The car wheels went into the sand 1 ½ inches. There was so much sand. My wife, Anna, and daughters, Libby and Anne were released from the hospital at 3:00 and then we are going in 7 ½ hours to "some kind of Rowena". We still haven't eaten dinner." [180]

Chapter 5
Hell for Those That Stayed Behind

Even though an unbelievable number of German-Russians emigrated, most still chose to stay near the Mother Volga. They were forced to adjust to the ever-tightening control of their daily lives by the Russian dynasty of the Romanov Czar[181]. Yet by 1914, there were still approximately 600,000 Germans living along the Volga River.

Russian (Stalin) Paranoia

Hitler and his Nazi party's rise to power in Germany worried Stalin about the loyalty of the Volga German-Russians and some feel that this might have lead to the purges of 1936 through 1938.[182] Actually, all of Russia suffered from these purges, not just the Volga German-Russians.

By 1938, the Stalinist terror had slaughtered over 3 million people (including all of Stalin's rivals and their families).[183] Russia had become crazy and paranoid, and the German language was forbidden except in the Volga region.

The Volga German Autonomous Soviet Socialist Republic Prime Minister, the Republic President, and other officials of the Volga government were arrested in 1937. They were not alone since by 1939, there were 18,572 German-Russians in "Corrective" Labor Camps.[184]

At the same time the Volga German-Russians were being imprisoned, they were also being praised. The *Moscow News* wrote in 1939:

"These people are demonstrating to the whole world what the industrious, gifted German people are capable of when they are free of the yoke of Capitalism."[185]

Also in 1939, a large-scale population exchange between Russia and Germany was planned following the Non-Aggression Pact signed between the Soviet Union and Germany. Many Germans from other parts of Russia did move back to areas closer to Germany. Almost none of the Volga German-Russians were able to move before Hitler broke the pact and invaded the Soviet Union on June 22, 1941.

When World War II began, the Volga German-Russians were the oldest, largest, and most densely populated group of Germans in the Soviet Union. The Volga German-Russians were trapped in a country that:

1) viewed them to be the same as Hitler and the Nazis[186]

2) was obsessed with the task that all Germans must be destroyed.

Stalin did not trust the loyalty of the 300,000 Volga German-Russians deep in Russian territory and quickly made plans for their immediate deportation after the wars' start. He needed some reason to "legitimize" his deportation plan. Within one month, the Soviet Government performed a series of large-scale "loyalty tests" in the Volga region.

In one of the tests, a detachment of Soviet security police disguised themselves as German soldiers and parachuted into the city of Engles. They wanted to learn the peoples response, and determine who the German-Russians were truly loyal to, Germany or Russia. Dressed as German soldiers and speaking fluent German, they were met with friendly greetings in some villages. In those disloyal villages, they killed the people and confiscated or destroyed their property. Not everyone was fooled,[187] but enough were. Stalin had his excuse for further action (as if he really needed one). He judged all German-Russians of the Volga Colonies "collectively guilty" of spying for the enemy[188] and of disloyalty.

Deported to Die

Moscow issued the Ukaz no. 21-160 order[189] declaring the banishment of all Volga German-Russians to Siberia on August 28, 1941. In this order, the government publicly announced that it was going to deport the entire German-Russian population living in the Volga region of over half a million men, women and children.[190] The order, signed by President Mikhail I. Kalinin, stated:

"According to trustworthy information received by the military authorities, there are among the German population living in the Volga area thousands and tens of thousands of diversionists and spies, who on a signal being given from Germany are to carry out sabotage in the area inhabited by the Germans of the Volga.

None of the Germans living in the Volga area has reported to the Soviet authorities the existence of such a large number of diversionists and spies among the Volga Germans; consequently the German population of the Volga area conceals enemies of the Soviet people and of the Soviet Authority in its midst.

In case of diversionist acts being carried out at a signal from German by German diversionists and spies in the Volga German Republic or in adjacent areas, and

bloodshed taking place, the Soviet Government will be obliged, according to the laws in force during the war period, to take punitive measures against the whole of the German population of the Volga.

In order to avoid undesirable events of this nature and to prevent serious bloodshed, the Presidium of the Supreme Soviet of the USSR have found it necessary to transfer the whole of the German population living in the Volga area into other areas, with the promise, however, that the migrants shall be allotted land and that they should be given assistance by the State in settling in the new areas.

For the purpose of resettlement, areas having much arable land in the Novosibirsk and Omsk Provinces, the Altai territory, Kazakhstan and other neighboring localities have been allotted.

In connection herewith the State Committee of Defense has been instructed to carry out urgently the transfer of all Germans of the Volga and to allot to the Germans of the Volga who are being transferred lands and domains in the new areas."[191]

A secret second order quickly followed. It described the procedures of how to conduct the deportations, and how to separate any remaining family heads from their families.[192]

Five days later on September 3,[193] the Russian NKVD moved in to the Volga German Republic to replace the existing Government by force. Their goal was to erase any trace of the German people. All German place names were replaced with Russian names. The NKVD surrounded German village with troops and went house-to-house to register them for deportation.[194] The Russian NKVD completed the operation 17 days later on September 20th.[195]

Sometimes, the German-Russians were not given the choice of deportation. The NKVD began mass shootings in many villages. Though the actual number is unknown, eyewitnesses reported tens of thousands of deaths.[196]

The order allowed deportees to take up to 2,000 pounds of personal property per family and an unlimited amount of money with them into exile. No cumbersome items were allowed. They were also required to bring one month's supply of food with them in order to feed themselves while on the journey.[197] Actually they were allowed to bring almost nothing.[198] Some families were given as little as five or ten minutes to pack up their belongings and food for the trip.[199]

Shortly after the September deportation, an official of the Russian Government named Volzhanin went to the now former Volga Colonies. His task was to select and classify the pedigree cattle that the German-Russians were forced to leave behind. He told the following:

"... when visiting many of the empty houses belonging to the German colonists he (Volzhanin) found stale bread and plates of soup covered with mold still set out on the tables, and in other homes saw articles of clothing which had been thrown on the floor, indicating the haste with which deportation had been carried out. The peasant farmsteads still contained cattle which had not been fed or milked for two weeks. A sow and her litter, dying of hunger, lay in one of the pigstys."[200]

And this was after the Russian NKVD and nearby Russian villagers had confiscated almost everything for themselves.

The deportees were herded to the nearest rail station and packed 40 to 60 persons into rail cattle cars.[201] The operation included 151 train convoys departing from 19 different rail stations.[202] The operation was handled just as one would handle beef cattle on the one-way trip to the slaughterhouse. In some cases, husbands, fathers and male children were separated and taken away never to be seen again.[203]

Deportation rules for each train specified a commander, a NKVD operative worker, twenty-one guards, a doctor, and two nurses, seven to nine cars for baggage, one medical car, and on train guard car.[204]

Russian mass hysteria had everyone hating the Germans, so there was no one there to protect their "rights" and the rules were not enforced. The Volga German-Russians were kept for two to three weeks in the unheated and filthy rail cars.[205] The insides of these rail cars had only a pail or hole for a toilet. The occupants soon became engulfed in a overwhelming stench of sweat, urine, feces and vomit.[206] Little drinking water, overcrowding and unsanitary conditions in the daytime searing summer heat and nighttime cold was what all were forced to endure.

During the two to three week trip into exile, many people (especially children) became ill with gastro-intestinal diseases, mange and measles[207].These horrible conditions quickly lead to death for many of the old, ailing, and young. Those still living were trapped with dead in the rail cars until the train stopped. The gut-wrenching stench of decaying corpses of what used to be your loved ones must have driven many crazy.

When the train finally did stop, those that were still strong enough quickly dug graves at the edge of the railroad for their dearly departed relatives rotting corpses.[208] In some cases,

94

the bodies were left in the overcrowded cattle wagons for weeks.[209] Winter arrived before most reached their banishment areas. With the ground frozen, the corpses of those that died froze solid and were stacked like cordwood on the edge of the tracks.[210] Most estimates indicate that close to 40% of the affected population perished during the trip.[211]

When they finally arrived at their banishment areas, they were considered by the Russians to be sub-humans. The Russians could use them or misuse them anyway they felt.[212] Everyone went into forced labor camps on arrival. Children under the age of 14 were put in orphanages. When they became 14, they too were put to work in the labor camps. Most of the camps were not constructed when the first Volga German-Russians arrived.

The German-Russians did whatever they had to in order to survive, often digging holes as shelter from the weather just as some of their ancestors had done 175 years earlier when they first arrived in the Volga River area.[213] Many that were lucky or strong enough to survive the horrific rail trip, soon perished in the service of the Russians.[214] Since most arrived in winter, the "lucky" survivors usually had inadequate clothing, no shelter, and no means to support themselves in temperatures as low as -40 deg F.[215]

Famine again stalked many of the German-Russian deportees. The Government told them that they could use food vouchers issued in exchange for their animals taken during the deportation for a small amount of grain. This was to feed them until they were placed into their assigned collective farms, But it was not until late 1941 that local Siberian authorities began accepting the vouchers.

For the first couple of months in exile, the deported German-Russians only had the food they brought. Some got more by bartering their few belongings with the local Russian population. The starving German-Russians willingly swapped valuable clothes, rugs and utensils for scraps of food. The local Russians felt no empathy for these enemy "Germans." The locals saw a chance to make a profit, and engaged in the regular cheating of German-Russian exiles in trade deals. [216]

The Soviet government knew that there was not enough food and resources in the deportation areas to keep the deportee population alive, and subsequently many Volga German-Russians only received starvation and death in Siberia.[217]

Here they formed a captive labor source to develop the agriculture, mining and forestry of these regions. Lack of shelter, food, warm clothing and medical care led to high death rates from not only starvation, but typhus, dysentery, gangrene and tuberculosis. It is estimated that about 20% or 250,000 German-Russians died during the 1940s from these diseases.[218]

The men and older boys that had not been killed were separated from their families, moved to the gulag as "soldiers" of a "working army" [219] or "Trud-Army," [220] and sent away to Siberia. Some of the men and boys from 16 to 55 were hauled off to work on the Trans-Siberian Railroad project where it was so cold that the men had to keep working in order not to freeze to death. Even so, many lost limbs that froze. Amputations must have been horrible as their was no medical care or painkillers.

Others were put on road construction, in the coalmines[221] of Kuzbas in the Kuznets hard-coal basin,[222] and gold mines[223] of northern Kazakhstan and the Urals, and timber felling [224] in the areas of the Kraslag, Viatlag and Usol'lag. [225] Few ever returned from the coalmines.

Women from 16 to 50 cut wood in the Siberian forests or also built railroads. If they did not meet their quota of cutting and trimming, they received no rations. [226] Some women and children went for "fishing" to Igarka, to settlements in the Turukhansk district, to Evenkia, to Taymyr and to settlements along the Angara River. [227]

What movement that was allowed was restricted to a limited zone always a few kilometers short of the nearest town. [228] Those that did survive could only live at the poverty level in settlements in Siberia, Kazakhstan, and other areas east of the Urals. They did not have the freedom to leave, and the penalty for leaving was 15-20 years of hard labor in the Gulag camps. [229]

By early 1942, the targeted population had expanded to include the entire German-Russian population of the USSR. By the end of 1942, over 850,000 German-Russians had been taken from their homes and exiled in Kazakhstan and Siberia. [230] By 1952, it is estimated that more than 1.2 million German people had been rounded up and dumped thousands of miles away in eastern and central Siberia or in the Central Asian republics. [231] That number does include the 439,000 Volga German-Russians deported to the Kazakhstan, Krasnoyarsk and Altai Krais, and Novosibiksk and Omsk areas. [232] Some of the Volga German-Russians that had been sent to the "Trud-Army" and still survived, were "released" from the camp zones in 1946. The "release" was in name only, as they were still sent into "internal exile" to the same places. [233]

By the end of World War II, the Soviet Government had eradicated or emptied 3,000 settlements, including those in the Volga area, across all of Soviet Russia of German-speaking citizens.[234] After WW II, those Volga German-Russians that were still alive were made to sign contracts with the Soviet government that promised they would never return to the Volga area.[235]

Further illustrating what the Volga German-Russians went through are the following three exile camp reports.

1) From the Colony of Donhof, Exile/Camp Report given by Frieda Andreas (daughter of Iwan Andreas). I selected this report because ANDREAS is one of my ancestor surnames possibly making this one of my relative's families.

"In September 1941 the ANDREAS family, Germans, was deported by the Soviets from the village of DENHOF, canton of BALZER, Autonomous Republic of the Volga Germans: Ivan ANDREAS (son of Jakob) - (1901-1962), his wife Jekaterina ANDREAS (daughter of Ivan) - (1901-1954), their children Andrej ANDREAS (son of Ivan), born in 1926, lives in Kazakhstan), Frieda ANDREAS (daughter of Ivan), born in 1927, lives in Krasnoyarsk, Emma ANDREAS (daughter of Ivan), born in 1928 and Eugenia ANDREAS (daughter of Ivan), born in 1938.

The journey to Siberia by train took about a month. Some of the deported persons were ordered to get off at SON station in Khakassia. The ANDREAS family (and another 8 families, all from DENHOF), were deported to the village of SNAMENKA in the BOGRADSK district / Khakassia.

Ivan ANDREAS suffered from asthma and, for that reason, was not called up into the "Trud-Army" in 1942. However, after 9 months of exile in SNAMENKA, in spring 1942, the Communists started to send all German families away to the North. The ANDREAS family got to the village of DVORETS, district of KEZHEMSK, on the river Angara. The exiled remained under military command until 1956."[236]

2) From the Colony of Straub, Exile/Camp Report given by Heinrich Bengel (son of Heinrich). I selected this report because Straub was the home village of many of my ancestors that lived in the Volga region. Had they not immigrated to the United States, this file might be about them.

"In September 1941 the Communists deported from the village of STRAUB, canton of KUKKUS, Autonomous Republic of the Volga Germans, the German farmer's family: BENGEL Heinrich, son of Peter, 1895-1957, BENGEL Kristina, daughter of Alexander, 1899-1970, BENGEL Anna, daughter of Heinrich, born in 1924, BENGEL Frieda, daughter of Heinrich, 1927-1948, BENGEL Heinrich, son of Heinrich, born in 1939.

On 28.10.41, the train with the exiled Germans was unloaded in Abakan, and they were taken on horseback to far-off villages. The BENGEL family came into exile in SAGAYSKOYE, a village in the district of KARATUSK. Among them were about 10 families from STRAUB: the WEISBROTs, the ROOTs, the SCHWABELLANTs, the GLEIMs and the DOOSes. The families of Kristina's brother, Daniel WINTER (son of Alexander), and his sister, Jekaterina BRAUSMAN (daughter of Alexander), were exiled to the village of KARATUS (district town).

Their father, Alexander WINTER, was deported to KLYUKVENNAYA station (today the town of UYAR), arrested there in autumn 1941 on section 58 and died in the NORILLag, as was heard by a roundabout way. Beginning 1942 Heinrich (son of Peter) and the 14-year-old Frieda were called up into the "Trud-Army". They came to KEMEROVO and both worked in the mine until 1946. There Frieda became ill with tuberculosis.

Next Anna was sent to the "Trud-Army", however, not to Krasnoyarsk, but to the BUMSTROY (paper works). Kristina was in luck: she was not sent to the "Trud-Army". In fact, mothers with little children were not supposed to be called up; nevertheless, this was done quite often. At the end of their term in the "Trud-Army" Henrich (son of Peter) and Frieda returned to the village of SAGAYSKOYE to live there in exile. Shortly afterwards, Frieda died from tuberculosis.

The elder son, Peter (son of Heinrich) BENGEL (born in 1921), served in the army from 1939. He finished the military college for artillery in Sumsk and became an officer; at the beginning of the war he had to go the front. In autumn 1941 he was taken out of the army, just as all the other Germans; but he was given a service record book, bearing the entry "at disposal for special duty".

He went to his family in Krasnoyarsk, without escort, and got to the BUMSTROY by accident (apparently, "Trud-armists" did not live behind barbed-wire fences there). When he mentioned his family name, he was immediately identified by his sister.

100

Later-on they sent Anna to the lumber industry in SHUMIKHU (today situated out of DIVNOGORSK), and in 1945 she was transferred to MINDERLINSK, to the NKVD "podkhoz" (an agricultural institution/farm that provided the nationalized firms in the towns with agricultural products, such as potatoes, vegetables, grain,...), which today is an "uchkhoz" (a mostly agricultural institution, where the apprentices learn about farming, cattle breeding, but also the repair of machines (plows, harrows,...), situated in the district of SUKHOBUSIMSK. After 1956 she stayed to live there."[237]

3) From the Colony of Donhof, Exile/Camp Report given by Klara Aab (daughter of Wilhelm Aab). I selected this report because AAB is also one of my ancestor surnames possibly making this one of my relative's families.

"Klara's family lived in DENHOF, a village in the canton of BALZER, Autonomous Republic of the Volga Germans. Her father, Wilhelm AAB (son of Friedrich), born in 1906, worked in the cotton weaving-mill in DENHOF (the rehabilitation documents mistakenly mention: solitary farmer).

He was arrested by the Communists on 02.11.37, sentenced on 11.11.37 in accordance with the decision of the Troyka of the NKVD of the Autonomous Republic of the Volga Germans and shot dead in BALZER on 13.11.37.

He was rehabilitated by the Saratov Regional Court on 31.07.1961. Klara Wilhelmovna familiarized herself with her father's court records No. OF-26326 in May 1990.

Actually, the file only shows one single entry "interrogations" - nothing else.

The file also mentions: SCHELER, Peter (son of Jakob), born in 1897, also arrested on 02.11.37 and shot dead on 13.11.37, as well as STOL, Heinrich (son of Heinrich). Wilhelm AAB's brother, Filipp AAB, born in 1899, worked as a joiner just in that factory.

He was arrested on 13.02.38, convicted of anti-Soviet agitation on 15.02.38 and shot dead in BALZER on 25.02.38. On the petition of the Saratov Regional Department of Public Prosecution he was rehabilitated as certified on 06.12.89.

On 17.09.41 the Soviets deported the following families from DENHOF: AAB Maria-Ekaterina (daughter of Wilhelm) (1908-1971), widow of Wilhelm AAB, her daughters Emma (born 1928), Klara (born 1930), her sons Viktor (born 1931) and Arthur (born 1937). BECHTOLD Ekaterina (approx. 1880-1943), mother of Wilhelm AAB, and her second husband BECHTOLD Georg (approx. 1875-1942).

AAB Elisabetha (born around 1902), widow of Filipp AAB, her daughter Ella (born 1936) and her sons Filipp (born around 1925) and Jakob (born around 1927). BECKER Wilhelm (born around 1906), his wife Maria (born 1901), their children Jewgenia (born around 1927), Frieda (born 1930), Karl (born 1935), Woldemar (born 1938), Erna (born 1941), Wilhelm (born around 1924).

They were en route by train for 17 days, then ordered to get off at SON station in Khakassia, North of Abakan; they were taken to the village of POTEKHINO in the district of BOGRADSK by rack wagons. There the five families lived in the former office building until spring. In January 1942 Wilhelm BECKER and his son Wilhelm were forced into the "Trud-Army". Shortly afterwards the son died.

The father returned in 1950 or 1951 and died a few years later. Then they obviously sent Filipp AAB to the KRASLag, in spring 1942 Jakob to IGARKA and the mother - to BASHKIRIA. Ella stayed with the grandmother and when she died, she was taken to an orphanage. Approximately in 1948 Filipp and Jakob returned and it was decided in the commander's office to take them to their mother.

Today she and Ella live in SALAVAT. In 1943 the families were sent to work in the timber industry of the SON region, 9 km away from SON station. This timber factory was transferred to the South in 1950, to the mountainous district of TASHTYPSK, to a village called MALY ARBAT, and the director insisted on having the Germans also transferred there. This demand was not rejected. The members of the AAB family live in Krasnoyarsk, members of the BECKER family in MALY ARBAT and the settlement of Arbasa."[238]

Chapter 6
Reversal of Deportations

In September 1955, fourteen years after the mass Volga German deportations occurred; First Secretary of the Communist Party of the Soviet Union Nikita Khrushchev began to eliminate numerous restrictions on the deportee's lives.[239]

Then on February 25, 1956, Khrushchev secretly condemned the deportations in his speech "On the Personality Cult and its Consequences"[240] (commonly known as the Secret Speech). This was a report to the 20th Congress of the Communist Party of the Soviet Union on February 25, 1956 by Soviet leader in which he denounced the past actions of former leader of the Soviet Union Josef Stalin as a violation of Leninist principles.[241]

While this literally shocked the 20th Congress, the Soviet government began the process of "De-Stalinization"[242] and reversed most of Stalin's deportations.[243]

Nikita Khrushchev [244]

It was only after this "De-Stalinization" did the living conditions of the deported German-Russians improve beyond the minimal survival level.[245]

Even after the Stalin era treason verdict against the Volga German-Russians was reversed, they continued to be controlled by numerous restrictions, such as the ban on return to their Volga homeland.[246] Full implementation of the "De-Stalinization" was slow and did not happen until 1964. [247]

The Soviet Government publicly issued an official decree (drafted on August 29, 1964) on January 5, 1965. After a little over 24 years, the truth comes out in this public announcement when it stated:

"Life has shown that sweeping accusations (namely that thousands and tens of thousands of diversionists and spies were to be found among the Volga Germans) were unfounded and represented an expression of despotic caprice, conditioned by the personal cult of Stalin. The successors of Stalin have now established that the overwhelming majority of the German population have in reality contributed through their work to the victory of the Soviet Union over German, and actively participated in the communist reconstruction during the postwar years." [248]

Under a special arrangement with the German government, Soviet Germans could immigrate to Germany, but this permission to return to their homelands only occurred after the disintegration of the Soviet Union in 1991.[249] After 1991, the Volga German-Russians (along with other deported groups such as the Crimean Tatars, and the ethnic Georgian Meskhs) were finally allowed to return en masse to their homelands.[250]

By the end of 1995, 1.4 million deported (or descendants of those deported) German-Russians had moved back to their original motherland of Germany[251] under the Federal Republic of Germany "Law of Return"[252] that recognizes the right of anyone with German ancestry to German citizenship[253]. There were 1.2 million more still living in Kazakhstan, Kyrgyzstan and the Russian Federation at the end of 1995.[254]

The Volga German-Russians were free to return back to Germany, or the Volga area of their ancestors, or so it seemed. Germany would accept them, but there was a language test to pass. There was also the fact that the individual people in Germany did not really want these "foreigners" back because they really were not real Germans anymore. Real Germans would not have left the motherland in the first place... So Germany was not the "home" that they expected, and being accepted by their native people was not to be easy.

However, there was always the possibility of returning to the Volga area of their ancestors. That was not to be. When the Volga German-Russians were ripped from their homes and deported in 1941, their productive villages and fields were left empty.

This did not last long and native Russians moved into the homes and took the property left behind for their own. They adopted the animals and worked the fields that they now owned. They knew that the former owners, those Germans, would never be back. The Soviet government had even renamed the villages so that all traces of the Germans had been erased.

When Communist Party Leader Mikhail Gorbachev began his perestroika (reconstruction), the "Volga German problem" became better known. In an effort to make things right, the Soviet government declared their intention of reestablishing the area of the former Volga German-Russians for their present day ancestors.

This would be accomplished by making a new Volga German Autonomous Republic or VGAR. This made a lot of sense to the former Volga German-Russians, who rightly viewed the forced deportation of their people as a terrible injustice. This would allow them to return home to their former villages and property to start a good life again.

The problem was that their villages were long gone. The buildings might still be there, but the village had been renamed with Russian names long ago with Russian families living in them for two or three generations. Those Russian families living in the area of the future VGAR believed rumors that they would be kicked out of their homes that they had lived in for generations, but would now revert to their previous owners when the Volga German-Russians returned.

Mass movements against the VGAR formed everywhere. They often used openly chauvinistic slogans and tended to equate the Volga German-Russians with the Nazis. Rumors of intentions to stop the "unwanted newcomers" by force circulated. The resistance proved to be too strong and the Soviet government dropped its' plan to build a new VGAR.

Even so, some former Volga German-Russians did resettle in the Volga region. They were not allowed to settle just anywhere, but were forced to live in "shipping containers" villages isolated from their former villages. After experiencing all the charms of life in these "container villages" among a hostile ethnic Russian population, many of them changed their minds and left. As word of their new life in the Volga spread, the number of Germans wanting to resettle just dried up. As a result, the percentage of ethnic German-Russians in the population of the Volga River area has remained quite low. Those Volga German-Russians that did stay dreamed of the creation of compact ethnic German settlements in the Volga region, the revival of the German language and culture, etc. They stayed hoping it would come true someday.[255]

On July 15, 1998, Robert Eksuzyan of Reuters News Service filed this story titled "Some Ethnic German Emigrants return to Russia. "About 400 ethnic German families are leaving Germany to return to the Volga region and western Siberia. Most cited their failure to learn German, and rules that restricted benefits to the ethnic Germans in the family as reasons to return. Most of those who returned were farmers."[256]

So where did the former Volga German-Russians that wanted to come back land up. By early 2000, the German government had tightened up the restrictions on those who wanted in to Germany. For example, immigrants from Russia could not choose their city of residence. If they did not cooperate, they were deprived of any financial help.

The language tests for immigrants have become incredibly difficult. "In the past one member of the family was required to speak German, while now everyone is required to pass a test, even the old men who had been prohibited to speak German," reported one immigrant.[257] More and more of them have failed in their assimilation efforts and have returned to the only home they know – back where they landed up after deportation in areas like Kazakhstan.

Information from a Balzer descendent, and former Kazakhstan resident, documents that many former Balzer family surname lines still survive in Kazakhstan. These are the surnames of individuals that were resettled there during the forced deportation, and of their descendants.

Among the families who are still represented include Engel, Haberman, Idt, Jakel, Kahm, Kaiser, Klaus, Kling, Lutz, Muller, Popp, Roth, Rutt, and Weber. Others that were from descended from those of other villages include Barthuly, Becker, Decker, Grasmuck, Klein, Meissinger, Ritter, Robertus and Schaffer.[258]

Deported German-Russians <u>enjoying</u> lunch while working the forests of "<u>Scenic</u>" Siberia 1948 [259]

Summary

In spite of all horrible challenges that the Volga Germans were faced with during their travels, they not only survived, but prospered. Some families traveled more than 10,000 miles over a 150-year period while searching for the right place to call home. Some families actually traveled back and inhabited the same areas that their ancestors inhabited thousands of years earlier. While the lucky ones voluntarily emigrated, all were forced by deportation to leave the Volga Colony areas. An amazing story of an amazing people!

Forgotten Volga German Grave & Tombstone in Warenburg Cemetery 2003 [260]

We cannot forget all they did for us!

Darrel P. Kaiser
2006

Bibliography

1941 Deportation, <http://members.rogers.com/kdee/History/10-Tribulations/Deportation>, accessed 20 July 2005

About St. Paul Lutheran Church of Port Huron, <http://www.lutheransonline.com/servlet/lo_ProcServ/dbpage=page&GID =0002700000107305978404781 6&PG=0002700000107305978412 6852>, accessed 18 July 2005

Alfano, Louis S, *Ellis Island 1892*, http://www.fortunecity.com/littleitaly/amalfi/100/ellis.htm

Alfano, Louis S, *The Immigration Experience*, <http://members.tripod.com/~L_Alfano/immig.htm>, accessed 21 May 2006

Ali, Tariq, *Trotsky For Beginners*,(Pantheon Books, New York, 1980)

A Volga German Homecoming, <http://www.lib.ndsu.nodak.edu/grhc/history_culture/history/volgagerman s.html>, accessed 11 April 2006

Bauer, Gottlieb, *Geschichte der deutschen Ansiedler an der Wolga*, (Sartov, Buchdruckerie "Energie", 1908)

Beine, Joe, *US Ports of Arrival*, <http://www.genesearch.com/ports.html>, accessed 20 May 2006

Bell, Diana, *116 Years of Volga Germans in Fresno*, <http://www.ahsgr.org/fresno/speech.html>, accessed 11 April 2006

Beratz, Gottlieb, *The German Colonies on the Lower Volga: Their Origin and Early Development* (Lincoln, NE: American Historical Society of Germans from Russia, 1991)

Conquest, Robert, *The Nation Killers: The Soviet Deportation of Nationalities*, (New York, NY: Macmillan Company, 1970)

113

Deportation, <http://www.stanford.edu/~skij/amintro.html>, accessed 21 September 2005

First Wave of German Immigration, <http://www.wisinfo.com/northwestern/ss/04/osh150/sesq_9430141.shtml >, accessed 9 April 2006

Fort Collins Public Library, *Local History Archive*, <http://library.ci.fort-collins.co.us/local_history/topics/Ethnic/German.htm>, accessed 9 April 2006

Geisinger, Adam, *From Catherine to Krushchev: The Story of Russia's Germans* (Winnipeg, Canada; Marian Press, 1974)

Genocide in the USSR, (Institute for the Study of the USSR, Munich, Germany, 1958)

German Americans in the Columbia River Basin, <http://www.vancouver.wsu.edu/crbeha/ga/ga.htm>, accessed 10 April 2006

Germans from Russia in Argentina, <http://comunidad.ciudad.com.ar/ciudadanos/herman/Volga/volga_eng.ht m>, accessed 10 April 2006

German Immigration, <http://www.houstonculture.org/tour/texas3b.html>, accessed 21 May 2006

Geschichte der Russlanddeutschen , <http://www.russlanddeutschegeschichte.de>, accessed 10 April 2006

Harms, Wilmer A., *Insights Into Russia,* (Journal of the AHSGR, Lincoln, NE, Volume 26, No. 2 Spring 2003)

Haynes, Emma S., *A History of the Volga Relief Society*, (AHSGR, Lincoln, NE, 1982)

Haynes, Emma Schwabenland, *Russian German History After 1917*, (80th Anniversary of the Free Evangelical Lutheran Cross Church 1892 – 1972, Fresno, Ca, 1972)

Hays City *Sentinel*, March 1, 1876

Hays City *Sentinel*, August 9, 1876

Heimatbuch der Deutschen aus Russland, 2000 (Landsmannschaft der Deutschen aus Rußland, Stuttgart, Germany, 2000)

History of Russia's Germans,
<http://www.russlanddeutschegeschichte.de/englisch1/luebeck_oranienba um.htm>, accessed 8 April 2006

History of the Russian-Germans,
<http://www.russlanddeutschegeschichte.de>, accessed 8 April 2006

History of the Soviet Union 1953-1985,
<http://en.wikipedia.org/wiki/History_of_the_Soviet_Union_%281953-1985%29>, accessed 8 April 2006

History of the Weitz Family,
<http://www.webbitt.com/weitz/history3.htm>, accessed 8 April 2006

Hoffman, Stefanie, *From Puppets of Stalin to Pawns of Hitler & Back Again: Experiences of Soviet Citizens of German Ethnicity During & After the Second World War*, (Journal of the AHSGR, Lincoln, NE, Volume 28, No. 1 Spring 2005)

Jan. 17, 1993, recorded by V.S Birger, Krasnoyarsk, "Memorial" society, <http://www.memorial.krsk.ru/eng/Dokument/Svidet/Bengel.htm>, accessed 9 April 2006

Kaiser, Philip, *Interview*, (Arbutus, Maryland, December 3, 2005)

Kazakhstan: Special Report on Ethnic Germans,
<http://www.irinnews.org/S_report.asp?ReportID=45321&SelectRegion= Central_Asia>, accessed 9 April 2006

Klein, Robert, *The Volga Germans*,
<http://www.webbitt.com/volga/lower/mrklein.htm>, accessed 9 April 2006

Kloberdanz, Timothy J., *The Germans from Russia: A Viable Ethnic Group or a Fading Phenomenon?*, (Journal of the AHSGR, Lincoln, NE, Volume 27, No. 1 Spring 2004)

Klooster, Karl, *Round the Roses*, (This Week Magazine, The Oregonian)

Koch, Fred, *The Volga Germans: in Russia and the Americas, from 1763 to the Present*, (University Park, PA: Pennsylvania State University Press, 1977)

Konigsberg: Our Family History Mid 1700's to Mid 1900's,
<http://home.att.net/~w.tomtschik/KDindex.html>, accessed 12 April 2006

Laing, Rev Francis S., *German-Russian Settlements in Ellis County, Kansas*, (The Commonwealth, January 15, 1876)

Lehmann, Heinz, *The German Canadians: 1750-1937. Immigration, settlement and culture*. Translated, edited and introduced by Gerhard P. Bassler (St. John's, NF: Jesperson Press, 1986)

Library of Congress, Prints and Photographs Division, Detroit Publishing Company Collection.

Mai, Brent Alan & Reeves-Marquardt, Dona, *German Migration to the Russian Volga (1764-1767)*, (AHSGR, Lincoln, NE, 2003)

Mai, Brent Alan, *Transport of the Volga Germans from Oranienbaum to the Colonies on the Volga 1766-1767*, AHSGR, Lincoln, NE, 1998)

May 28, 1990, recorded by V.S. Birger, "Memorial" Society, Krasnoyarsk ,
<http://www.memorial.krsk.ru/eng/Dokument/Svidet/Aab.htm>, accessed 9 April 2006

McWilliams, Rita, *We the People: Germans*, (Maryland Magazine (Autumn) 1990): pp 26-33

Migration News,
<http://migration.ucdavis.edu/mn/more.php?id=1602_0_4_0>, accessed 11 April 2006

Miller, Patrice, *Volga Germans*, <http://www.webbitt.com/volga>, accessed 11 April 2006

Miller, Patrice, *Canada Settlement List*,
<http://www.webbitt.com/volga/home.html>, accessed 19 September 2006

Nebraska Ancestree,
<http://www.rootsweb.com/~nesgs/Ancestree/vol02/v02n3p127.htm>, accessed 9 April 2006

Niessner, Roswita, *The Moscow Consistorial District*, (Journal of the American Historical Society of Germans' from Russia, Lincoln, NE, Volume 26, No. 2 Summer 2003)

Nikita Krushchev, Photographer unknown,
<http://www.dictatorofthemonth.com/Kruschev/pictures_of_kruschev.htm>, accessed 30 August 2006

Norka A German Colony in Russia,
<http://www.volgagermans.net/norka/Norka_emigration.htm>, accessed 11 April 2006

Nov. 28, 1991, recorded by V.S. Birger, Krasnoyarsk, "Memorial" Society
<http://www.memorial.krsk.ru/eng/Dokument/Svidet/Andreas.htm>, accessed 11 April 2006

On the Personality Cult and Its Consequences,
<http://en.wikipedia.org/wiki/On_the_Personality_Cult_and_its_Conseque nces>, accessed 12 April 2006

Oshkosh, <http://members.tripod.com/highholder/oshkosh.htm>, accessed 11 April 2006

Packet Boats,
<http://www.postalheritage.org.uk/history/transport/water_packetboats.ht
ml>, accessed 15 July 2005

Parks - Castle Clinton National Monument,
<http://genealogy.about.com/gi/dynamic/offsite.htm?zi=1/XJ&sdn=geneal
ogy&zu=http%3A%2F%2Fwww.gorp.com%2Fgorp%2Fresource%2FUS_
NM%2Fny_castl.HTM>, accessed 25 May 2006

Pfeifer, Leona, *The Life of the German Woman in Russia,* (Journal of the
American Historical Society of Germans from Russia, Lincoln, NE,
Volume 26, No. 2 Spring 2003)

Pleve, Igor R., *The German Colonies on the Volga: The Second Half of the
Eighteenth Century,* (AHSGR, Lincoln, NE, 2001)

Pohl, Otto, *Ethnic Cleansing in the USSR, 1937-1949,* (Westport, CT:
Greenwood Press, 1999)

Pohl, J. Otto, <http://jpohl.blogspot.com/2005/08/in-our-hearts-we-felt-
sentence-of.html>, accessed 4 July 2006

Popp, Victor & Dening, Nicolás, *Los Alemanes del Volga,* (1977),
<http://www.alemanesvolga.com.ar/libros/l3.html>, accessed 21 July 2006

Population Transfer in the Soviet Union,
<http://en.wikipedia.org/wiki/Population_transfer_in_the_Soviet_Union>,
accessed 9 April 2006

Public Health Service, National Archive/Photo Researchers, Inc.

Rath, George, *Emigration from Germany through Poland and Russia to
the U.S.A.,* (1969)

Riffel, Jakob, *Die Russlanddeutschen insbesondere die Wolgadeutschen
am La Plata,* (Selbstverlag des Verfassers, Argentina)

Right of Return,
<http://en.wikipedia.org/wiki/Right_of_return#Germany>, accessed 12
April 2006

Roll, Mitch, *German-Russian Volga Area Map*, (Dallas, Texas)

Ruppenthal, J. C., *The German Element in Central Kansas*, (KHC, v. 13,
1913-1914)

Russia's Ethnic Germans Who Live in Germany Want Back Home,
<http://english.pravda.ru/society/2002/08/28/35468.html>, accessed 11
April 2006

Sallet, Richard, *Russlanddeutsche Siedlungen in den Vereinigten Staaten,*
(German-American Historical Review, Chicago, 1931)

Saskatchewan Time Lines,
<http://www.rootsweb.com/~cansk/Saskatchewan/Timeline-Sk.html>,
accessed 9 April 2006

Saul, Norman, *Concord and Conflict, The United States and Russia, 1867-
1914*, pp. 335-355

Schwabenland, Emma, *A History of the Volga Relief Society* (AHSGR,
Lincoln, NE, 1982)

Smith, Juliana, *The Port of New York :Gateway to America,*
<http://genealogy.about.com/gi/dynamic/offsite.htm?zi=1/XJ&sdn=geneal
ogy&zu=http%3A%2F%2Fwww.ancestry.com%2Flibrary%2Fview%2Fc
olumns%2Fcompass%2F2845.asp>, accessed 24 May 2006

S.S. Lituania, <http://www.davefox73.com/images/Lituania_Lan.jpg>,
accessed 11 April 2006

Sulzberger, Cyrus L., Wireless to The New York Times from Moscow,
Monday, September 8, 1941

The Adolph Family, (Journal of the AHSGR, Winter 1988, Lincoln, NE,
1988)

The deportation from the Autonomous Republic of the Volga-Germans (September 1941), <http://www.memorial.krsk.ru/eng/Exile/062.htm>, accessed 11 April 2006

THE DIARY OF JOSEPH MARECEK, <http://familytreemaker.genealogy.com/users/s/c/h/Leah-B-Schniers/BOOK-0001/0003-0001.html>, accessed 20 May 2006

The German Colonies on the Volga River-Deportation, <http://www.volgagermans.net/volgagermans/Volga%20German%20Deportation.htm>, accessed 12 April 2006

The Jamestown Foundation Prism, (Volume 4, Issue 10, May 15, 1998), <http://www.jamestown.org/publications_details.php?volume_id=5&issue_id=276&article_id=313>, accessed 21 January 2006

The Migration of the Russian Germans to Kansas, <http://www.kshs.org/publicat/khq/1974/graphics/74_1_santafe_poster.jpg>, accessed 9 April 2006

The Palouse, <http://www.idahoptv.org/productions/idahoportrait/tour/palousetour.html>, accessed 10 April 2006

The Scouts, <http://www.fhsu.edu/forsyth_lib/VolgaGerman/Scouts.jpg>, accessed 9 April 2006

The Statue of Liberty – Ellis Island Foundation, Inc, <http://www.ellisisland.org>, accessed 5 April 2006

The Volga Germans-Those that stayed behind, <http://members.aol.com/RAToepfer/webdoc8x.htm>, accessed 10 April 2006

Torture in Russian Prisons, <www.rusalma.org>, accessed 17 September 2006

USA Settlement List, <http://www.webbitt.com/volga/usa-settle-list.html>, accessed 15 July 2005

Village of Balzer,
<http://www.femling.com/gen/balzer/balzer.htm#Village%20of%20Balzer >, accessed 10 April 2006

Volga German, <http://www.volgagerman.net/>, accessed 10 April 2006

Volga German Autonomous Soviet Socialist Republic, <http://volga-german-autonomous-soviet-socialist-republic.biography.ms/>, accessed 1 April 2006

Volga Germans United States, <http://www.webbitt.com/volga/usa.html>, accessed 10 April 2006

White, Sharon, *German Tombstone in Warenburg Cemetery in 2003*

Williams, Hattie Plum, *The Czar's Germans*, (AHSGR, Lincoln, NE, 1975)

Züge, Gottlieb, *The Russian Colonist or Christian Gottlieb Züge's Life in Russia with a Description of Russian Life and Habits in Their Asiatic Provinces* (Germany 1802)

End Notes

[1] Author created

[2] Williams, Hattie Plum, *The Czar's Germans*, p. 106

[3] Pleve, Igor R., *The German Colonies on the Volga: The Second Half of the Eighteenth Century*, p. 106

[4] Bauer, Gottlieb, *Geschichte der deutschen Ansiedler an der Wolga*, p.19

[5] Williams, Hattie Plum, *The Czar's Germans*, p. 56

[6] *Packet Boats*

[7] Williams, Hattie Plum, *The Czar's Germans*, p. 56

[8] *History of Russia's Germans*

[9] Williams, Hattie Plum., *The Czar's Germans*, p. 107

[10] Geisinger, Adam, *From Catherine to Krushchev: The Story of Russia's Germans*, p. 10

[11] *Geschichte der Russlanddeutschen*

[12] ibid

[13] Beratz, Gottlieb, *The German Colonies on the Lower Volga*, pp. 50-51

[14] ibid

[15] Haynes, Emma S., *A History of the Volga Relief Society*, p.17

[16] Beratz, Gottlieb, *The German Colonies on the Lower Volga*, pp. 51, 54

[17] ibid, p. 55

[18] ibid

[19] Author created

[20] *Geschichte der Russlanddeutschen*

[21] Roll, Mitch, *German-Russian Volga Area Map*

[22] Miller, Patrice, *Volga Germans*

[23] Photographer unknown

[24] Geisinger, Adam, *From Catherine to Krushchev: The Story of Russia's Germans*, p. 15

[25] Williams, Hattie Plum., *The Czar's Germans*, p. 111

[26] Haynes, Emma S., *A History of the Volga Relief Society*, p.17

[27] Züge, Gottlieb, *The Russian Colonist or Christian Gottlieb Züge's Life in Russia*

[28] Haynes, Emma S., *A History of the Volga Relief Society*, p.17

[29] Pfeifer, Leona, *The Life of the German Woman in Russia*, p.21

[30] Mai, Brent Allen, *Transport of the Volga Germans from Oranienbaum to the Colonies on the Volga*

[31] Mai, Brent Alan; Reeves-Marquardt, Dona, *German Migration to the Russian Volga (1764-1767)*, p. iii

[32] Pfeifer, Leona, *The Life of the German Woman in Russia*, p.21

[33] Beratz, Gottlieb, *The German Colonies on the Lower Volga*, p. 80

[34] ibid, p. 81

[35] ibid, p. 80
[36] Author created
[37] Beratz, Gottlieb, *The German Colonies on the Lower Volga*, p. 138
[38] ibid, p. 129
[39] ibid
[40] Author created
[41] Beratz, Gottlieb, *The German Colonies on the Lower Volga,*, pp. 129-130
[42] ibid, p. 130
[43] *Torture in Russian Prisons*
[44] Niessner, Roswita, *The Moscow Consistorial District*, p.1
[45] Author created
[46] Williams, Hattie Plum, The Czar's Germans, p.173
[47] Haynes, Emma S., *A History of the Volga Relief Society*, p.24
[48] ibid
[49] Hoffman, Stefanie, *From Puppets of Stalin to Pawns of Hitler & Back Again*, p.10
[50] Author unknown
[51] Harms, Wilmer A., *Insights Into Russia*, p.16
[52] Sallet, Richard, *Russlanddeutsche Siedlungen in den Vereinigten Staaten*, pp. 31-49
[53] Williams, Hattie Plum, The Czar's Germans, p. 176
[54] ibid
[55] Riffel, Jakob, *Die Russlanddeutschen insbesondere die Wolgadeutschen am La Plata,*pp.18-21,32-38
[56] Author created
[57] *Germans from Russia in Argentina*
[58] Popp, Victor & Dening, Nicolás, *Los Alemanes del Volga*
[59] Author created
[60] *History of the Russian-Germans*
[61] Saul, Norman, *Concord and Conflict, The United States and Russia, 1867-1914*, pp. 335-355
[62] *Konigsberg : Our Family History Mid 1700's to Mid 1900's, bid*
[63] *The Migration of the Russian Germans to Kansas*
[64] Bell, Diana, *116 Years of Volga Germans in Fresno*
[65] Author created
[66] Bell, Diana, *116 Years of Volga Germans in Fresno*
[67] *USA Settlement List*
[68] Haynes, Emma S., A History of the Volga Relief Society, p.25
[69] *USA Settlement List*
[70] Fort Collins Public Library, *Local History Archive*
[71] Author created
[72] *USA Settlement List*

[73] *The Palouse*
[74] Author created
[75] *USA Settlement List*
[76] *Volga Germans United States*
[77] Klein, Robert, *The Volga Germans*
[78] Author created
[79] *USA Settlement List*
[80] Author created
[81] *USA Settlement List*
[82] *The Scouts*
[83] *Volga German*
[84] Laing, Rev Francis S., *German-Russian Settlements in Ellis County, Kansas,* p. 494
[85] Hays City *Sentinel*, August 9, 1876
[86] Hays City *Sentinel*, March 1, 1876
[87] *A Volga German Homecoming*
[88] ibid
[89] ibid
[90] ibid
[91] ibid
[92] Ruppenthal, J. C., *The German Element in Central Kansas,* pp. 513-553
[93] *A Volga German Homecoming*
[94] Author created
[95] *USA Settlement List*
[96] Author created
[97] *USA Settlement List*
[98] *About St. Paul Lutheran Church of Port Huron*
[99] Author created
[100] *USA Settlement List*
[101] Author created
[102] *USA Settlement List*
[103] Klein, Robert, *The Volga Germans*
[104] Author created
[105] *USA Settlement List*
[106] Author created
[107] Klein, Robert, *The Volga Germans*
[108] *Nebraska Ancestree*
[109] *USA Settlement List*
[110] Author created
[111] *History of the Weitz Family*
[112] Author created
[113] *USA Settlement List*

[114] Author created
[115] *USA Settlement List*
[116] Author created
[117] *USA Settlement List*
[118] Klein, Robert, *The Volga Germans*
[119] Author created
[120] *USA Settlement List*
[121] *Norka A German Colony in Russia*
[122] Klooster, Karl, *Round the Roses*
[123] *Norka A German Colony in Russia*
[124] Rath, George, *Emigration from Germany through Poland and Russia to the U.S.A*
[125] Klooster, Karl, *Round the Roses*
[126] *Norka A German Colony in Russia*
[127] Author created
[128] Rath, George, Emigration from Germany through Poland and Russia to the U.S.A.
[129] *USA Settlement List*
[130] Author created
[131] *USA Settlement List*
[132] Author created
[133] *USA Settlement List*
[134] Author created
[135] *German Americans in the Columbia River Basin*
[136] *USA Settlement List*
[137] *Oshkosh*
[138] *History of the Weitz Family*
[139] *Oshkosh*
[140] *First Wave of German Immigration*
[141] *History of the Weitz Family*
[142] Author created
[143] *USA Settlement List*
[144] Author created
[145] Lehmann, Heinz, *The German Canadians: 1750-1937. Immigration, settlement and culture.*, p. 118
[146] *Saskatchewan Time Lines*
[147] Miller, Patrice, *Canada Settlement List*
[148] Author created
[149] Miller, Patrice, *Canada Settlement List*
[150] Niessner, Roswita, *The Moscow Consistorial District*, p.1
[151] Photographers unknown
[152] Kaiser, Philip, *Interview*

[153] *The Adolph Family,* p. 37
[154] Photographer unknown
[155] *S.S. Lituania*
[156] *The Statue of Liberty – Ellis Island Foundation, Inc*
[157] Beine, Joe, *US Ports of Arrival*
[158] *Parks - Castle Clinton National Monument*
[159] Library of Congress, Prints and Photographs Division, Detroit Publishing Company Collection
[160] ibid
[161] Alfano, Louis S., *The Immigration Experience*
[162] ibid
[163] Alfano, Louis S, *Ellis Island 1892*
[164] Photographer unknown
[165] ibid
[166] ibid
[167] Library of Congress, Prints and Photographs Division, Detroit Publishing Company Collection
[168] ibid
[169] ibid
[170] Photographer unknown
[171] Library of Congress, Prints and Photographs Division
[172] Smith, Juliana, *The Port of New York :Gateway to America*
[173] Library of Congress, Prints and Photographs Division
[174] ibid
[168] ibid
[176] ibid
[177] Public Health Service, National Archive
[178] McWilliams, Rita, *We the People: Germans*
[179] German Immigration
[180] *THE DIARY OF JOSEPH MARECEK*
[181] Harms, Wilmer A., *Insights Into Russia,* p.16
[182] Pohl, Otto, *Ethnic Cleansing in the USSR, 1937-1949,* p.30
[183] Ali, Tariq, *Trotsky for Beginners,* pp.160-161
[184] Pohl, Otto, *Ethnic Cleansing in the USSR, 1937-1949,* p.30
[185] Koch, Fred, *The Volga Germans: in Russia and the Americas, from 1763 to the Present,* p.260
[186] Pohl, Otto, *Ethnic Cleansing in the USSR, 1937-1949,* p.36
[187] ibid
[188] *1941 Deportation*
[189] Pohl, J. Otto
[190] ibid
[191] Conquest, Robert, *The Nation Killers. The Soviet Deportation of Nationalities,*

pp.62-63

[192] Sulzberger, Cyrus L.

[193] *1941 Deportation*

[194] Pohl, Otto, *Ethnic Cleansing in the USSR, 1937-1949*, p.36

[195] Pohl, J. Otto

[196] *Deportation*

[197] Pohl, Otto, *Ethnic Cleansing in the USSR, 1937-1949*, p.36

[198] Geisinger, Adam, *From Catherine to Krushchev: The Story of Russia's Germans*, p.315

[199] *1941 Deportation*

[200] Genocide in the USSR, (Institute for the Study of the USSR, Munich, Germany, 1958): pp.50 - 51

[201] Geisinger, Adam, *From Catherine to Krushchev: The Story of Russia's Germans*, p.315

[202] *1941 Deportation*

[203] Geisinger, Adam, *From Catherine to Krushchev: The Story of Russia's Germans*, p.315

[204] Pohl, Otto, *Ethnic Cleansing in the USSR, 1937-1949*, p.36

[205] Kloberdanz, Timothy J., *The Germans from Russia: A Viable Ethnic Group or a Fading Phenomenon?*, p.19

[206] Pohl, J. Otto

[207] ibid

[208] Kloberdanz, Timothy J., *The Germans from Russia: A Viable Ethnic Group or a Fading Phenomenon?*, p.19

[209] *1941 Deportation*

[210] Kloberdanz, Timothy J., *The Germans from Russia: A Viable Ethnic Group or a Fading Phenomenon?*, p.19

[211] *1941 Deportation*

[212] Kloberdanz, Timothy J., *The Germans from Russia: A Viable Ethnic Group or a Fading Phenomenon?*, p.19

[213] *Kazakhstan: Special Report on Ethnic Germans*

[214] Kloberdanz, Timothy J., *The Germans from Russia: A Viable Ethnic Group or a Fading Phenomenon?*, p.19

[215] *1941 Deportation*

[216] Pohl, J. Otto

[217] *Deportation*

[218] Pohl, J. Otto

[219] *Kazakhstan: Special Report on Ethnic Germans*

[220] *The deportation from the Autonomous Republic of the Volga-Germans (September 1941)*

[221] *The Volga Germans-Those that stayed behind*

[222] *The deportation from the Autonomous Republic of the Volga-Germans*

128

(September 1941)
[223] Deportation
[224] The Volga Germans-Those that stayed behind
[225] The deportation from the Autonomous Republic of the Volga-Germans
(September 1941)
[226] The Volga Germans-Those that stayed behind
[227] The deportation from the Autonomous Republic of the Volga-Germans
(September 1941)
[228] 1941 Deportation
[229] ibid
[230] Pohl, J. Otto
[231] 1941 Deportation
[232] Population Transfer in the Soviet Union
[233] The deportation from the Autonomous Republic of the Volga-Germans
(September 1941)
[234] Kloberdanz, Timothy J., The Germans from Russia: A Viable Ethnic Group or
a Fading Phenomenon?, p.19
[235] Volga German Autonomous Soviet Socialist Republic
[236] Nov. 28, 1991
[237] Jan. 17, 1993
[238] May 28, 1990
[239] The German Colonies on the Volga River-Deportation
[240] Population Transfer in the Soviet Union
[241] On the Personality Cult and Its Consequences
[242] History of the Soviet Union 1953-1985
[243] Population Transfer in the Soviet Union
[244] Nikita Krushchev
[245] Pohl, J. Otto
[246] Kazakhstan: Special Report on Ethnic Germans
[247] The German Colonies on the Volga River-Deportation
[248] Haynes, Emma Schwabenland, Russian German History After 1917, pp.142 –
145
[249] The German Colonies on the Volga River-Deportation
[250] Population Transfer in the Soviet Union
[251] The German Colonies on the Volga River-Deportation
[252] Right of Return
[253] Volga German Autonomous Soviet Socialist Republic
[254] The German Colonies on the Volga River-Deportation
[255] The Jamestown Foundation Prism
[256] Migration News
[257] Russia's Ethnic Germans Who Live in Germany Want Back Home
[258] Village of Balzer

[259] *Heimatbuch der Deutschen aus Russland, 2000*
[260] White, Sharon, *German Tombstone in Warenburg Cemetery in 2003*

Books by Darrel P. Kaiser
www.DarrelKaiserBooks.com

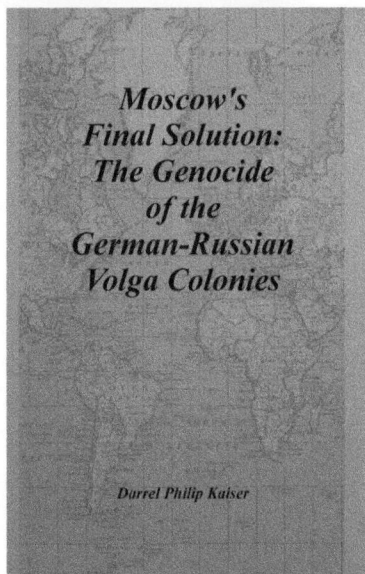

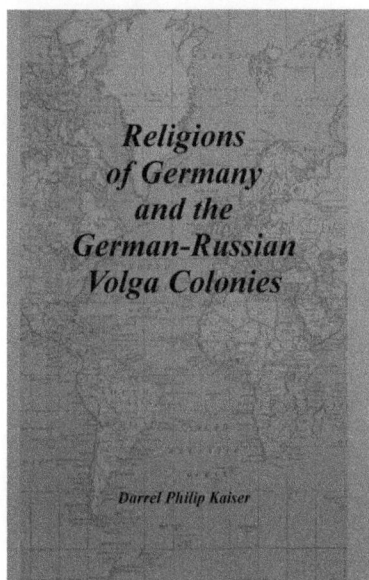

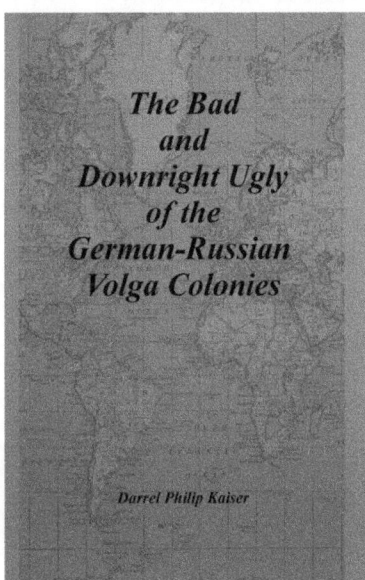

Origin & Ancestors
Families
Karle & Kaiser
of the
German-Russian Volga Colonies

Adolf	Heyimann	Nдив
Andreas	Hieronymus	Rudolph
App	Horn	Schaeffer
Arnz	Ischudi	Scherer
Becker	Kaiser	Schiller
Bopp	Karle	Schmiedt
Barbach	Köhler	Schneider
Dagenheim	Krämer	Schütz
Foht	Lieders	Simon
Freund	Maurer	Seitz
Geringer	Michel	Trieber
Grün	Neff	Trippel
Hartt	Neumann	Vogt
Heiland	Nicolausen	Werner
Hermann	Nillmeyer	Will
Hess	Popp	Zeichmann

Darrel Philip Kaiser

Moscow's
Final Solution:
The Genocide
of the
German-Russian
Volga Colonies

Darrel Philip Kaiser

Religions
of Germany
and the
German-Russian
Volga Colonies

Darrel Philip Kaiser

The Bad
and
Downright Ugly
of the
German-Russian
Volga Colonies

Darrel Philip Kaiser

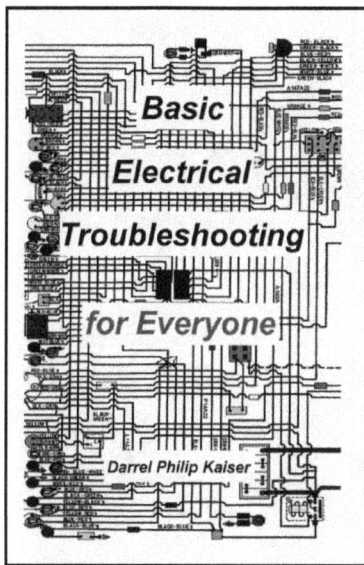

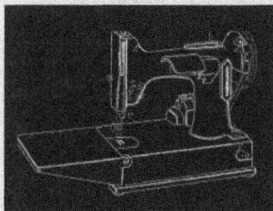

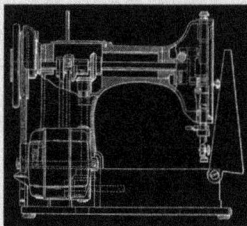

Books by Darrel P. Kaiser
www.DarrelKaiserBooks.com

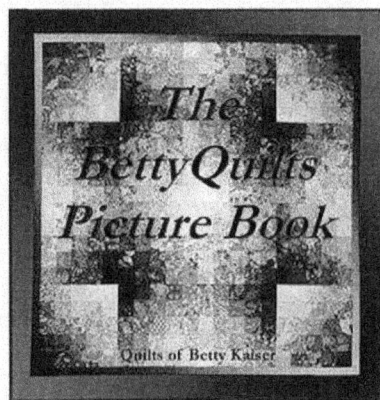

before the
Featherweight

Sewhandy
Volume 1
History

Darrel P. Kaiser

before the
Featherweight

Sewhandy
Volume 2
Maintenance
& Repair

Darrel P. Kaiser

Logical
Sewing Machine
Troubleshooting

ALL BRANDS

ANTIQUE - COMPUTER

for Everyone

Darrel Philip Kaiser

The
BettyQuilts
Picture Book

Quilts of Betty Kaiser

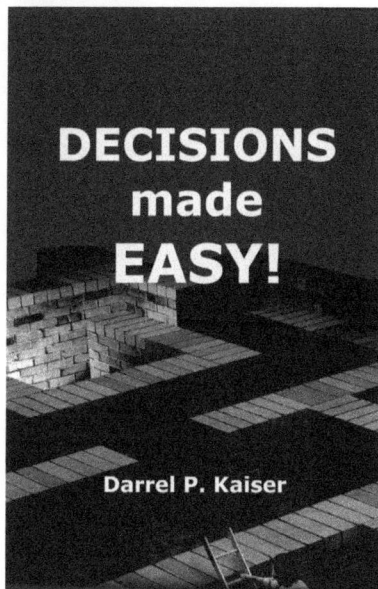

www.ingramcontent.com/pod-product-compliance
Lightning Source LLC
Chambersburg PA
CBHW030019290326
41934CB00005B/404